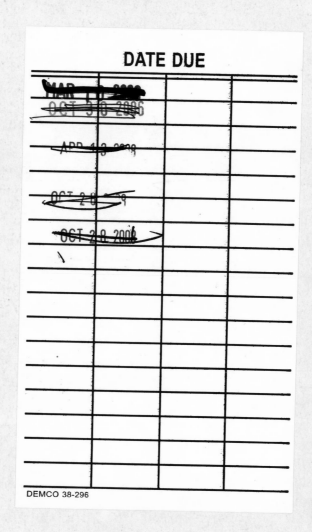

DATE DUE

DEMCO 38-296

ART NOUVEAU DRAWINGS

ART NOUVEAU DRAWINGS

Petr

Wittlich

Alfons Mucha
Aubrey Beardsley
Odilon Redon
Edvard Munch
Jan Preisler
František Bílek
Alfred Kubin
František Kupka
Auguste Rodin
Gustav Klimt
Egon Schiele

OCTOPUS BOOKS

First published 1974 by
Octopus Books Limited
59 Grosvenor Street, London W1
Reprinted 1975
Translated by Till Gottheiner
Graphic design by Aleš Krejča

© 1974 Artia, Prague
Text © 1974 Petr Wittlich
Illustrations: Nos 1—10 © 1974 Jiří Mucha, Prague;
frontispiece and Nos 25—28 © 1974 Rolf Stenersen,
Kunstforlag A/S., Oslo; Nos 35—39 © 1974 Jan
Kudláček, Prague; Nos 40—42 © 1974 mit Ge-
nehmigung der Nymphenburger Verlagshandlung
GmbH., München; Nos 43—46 © 1974, Copyright by
A.D.A.G.P. Paris, and COSMOPRESS, Geneva; Nos
47—49 © 1974 Copyright by S.P.A.D.E.M., Paris.

ISBN 0 7064 0297 9

Printed in Czechoslovakia

2/02/12/51

CONTENTS

Art, at the turn of the 19th and 20th centuries, grew under circumstances, which, in the context of the history of art, can be likened to the situation in which European art advanced from Antiquity to the Middle Ages.[1] Such a comparison can, of course, only be an approximate one, in view of the differing parameters of contents, and since the time dimensions of this recent development are much shorter. But the fact remains that, in the brief period from the eighties of the 19th century to the beginning of the First World War, European art underwent revolutionary changes, which put an end to the predominance of the realistic manner, that is, of pictures conceived in terms introduced and basically elaborated by the Italian Renaissance, and, at the same time, laid art open to views that regarded its share in the human consciousness of the world in an entirely different, unconventional manner.

At first glance, art around 1900 appears as a mosaic of many forms. The extreme individualism of this period, proclaimed by critical thinkers such as Nietzsche, enjoyed quite exceptional authority, and evoked immediate response among the growing, though socially still unsettled community of artists. It was not merely an attractive attitude. It also promised expression for the profound need of the artist to share in world events. The turn of the century was undoubtedly a period of overall social and spiritual crisis. Major shifts in the social system, caused by the process of industrialization, shook its existing structure; these changes complicated not only political conditions but had profound effects on the world of philosophy and imagination. It was as though cracks appeared in the accepted, familiar and matter-of-fact face of objects and thoughts, to release heady and bewitching ideas which formed conceptual leaps from momentary experiences to the depths of history and the human soul, and to imagined utopias of the future.

This romantic spirit, which blossomed once more among artists, differed at core, however, from original Romanticism. Scepticism, convinced of the catastrophically tragic state of affairs, was its omnipresent companion. This ever-changing, uncertain basis underlay all the authentic art that was created in the decisive period around 1900, and tinged it with melancholy. The fragility of its dreams, and their fairy-tale illusions, were as insubstantially rooted as a house of cards built on sand. But it also gave rise to a more vital undercurrent that often etched turbulence and emotion onto the stylized surface, conquering all efforts to subdue it by means of ornament, and substantially contributing to the internal structure of modern art as a value that was not simply that of an artistic mode alone. It stimulated the basic changing of art into a constant striving, by which Man's profound longing for freedom is given back to the world of unstable reality, and through which it acquires the necessary structures for its self-realization.

Today we can draw a figurative triangle as a paradigm of this art as a whole, putting its major aspects, as they began to form, into structural interconnections. At its apexes we find the three most typical and prophetic aspects of art around 1900.

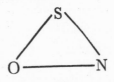

One apex is formed by *Naturalism* as a trend that linked up with painting's modern development towards an optical sharpness of perception resulting from an awakened and steadily growing appreciation of detail. And not only detail in the sense of a narrative comprehension of reality, but expressly in connection with the modern course towards empirical, first-hand knowledge of natural and human reality. We should not overlook the major influence of literature in this respect, particularly of works on the natural sciences, and of fiction, e.g. the influence of Zola's novels, which reflect his admiration for Manet and the Impressionists. But apart from the influences of these wider cultural areas, the main source of the naturalistic trend was, undoubtedly, the development of art itself, which, theoretically stimulated in the middle of the 19th century, e.g. by Ruskin's theory of the 'innocent eye', turned into the quasi-materialist painting of the Impressionists. The Impressionists, indeed, freed art from the bonds of the long-established and already academic allegorism, which once had linked painting and poetry in an important sense, but which, in the 19th century, in most cases represented no more than a conventional social function, where art was thought of merely as a hired means of social representation and decoration; and often as a mere veil for a variety of pseudo-cultural parvenuism, at both national and private level. In contrast to the salon art of the 19th century, the Impressionists turned the spectator's attention to the common, everyday world of natural and city scenery, to life seen no longer through the spectacles of late Romantic nationalism or pietism, but seen directly in its natural energy. The Impressionists chose cosmic sunlight as their main theme. This led to the growing liberation of colour in the picture, and a gradually developing feeling for the unity of the picture with the world as it truly is. The pictures of Claude Monet's late period culminated in the almost mystical sensation of their merging with the essence of world being through the eyes. The Pointillist re-evaluation of Impressionism by Seurat showed yet another possibility, namely how a consistent visual system of form could be built up on the newly acquired status of 'immediate' art.

Seurat's solution, which met with wide response as early as the eighties of the 19th century, showed how the art of the end of the century clamoured for a new style. The Impressionists' serenity and ease could clearly not cover the entire scope of the functions that art plays in the life of society.

To this requirement is related the second apex of our triangle which might be termed that of *decorative Ornamentation*. At the turn of the century, the concept of style was still closely linked to the problem of ornament. Ornament was even considered the basis of all art, insofar as it laid claim to broader social applicability. This position of ornament in the scale of values was temporarily strengthened by the application of Kant's concept of pure beauty, valid per se, to decorative art. This concept remained attractive until abstract art was invented. The 19th century persistently searched for an expression of its own. Being proud of scientific progress and technical mastery, it wished to install even in the arts a style of general validity; but, hypnotized by period historicism, it merely repeated and amassed old recipes. This situation was most pronounced in architecture and the arts and crafts. A new solution was reached only when polyhistoricism receded. The nineties witnessed the birth and rapid spread of a new style, which could lay claim to being original. French *Art Nouveau*, German *Jugendstil*, Austrian *Sezession* were only the most striking labels on the magic bottle which when opened let forth the lively genie of a new international style. With its charming curves and arabesques it changed the architecture and decorative articles of the entire civilized world within the short space of a few years.

R. Schmutzler has shown how the sources of this new ornamental style came into being in England, and how the roots of this plant, which was to blossom into the dazzling graphic work of Aubrey Beardsley, stretch back to the work of the visionary William Blake.[2] The lesson taught by England was undeniably stimulating to artists on the Continent, but one should not overlook some essential sources of local character which can be found, e.g. in early drawings by one of the protagonists of the new style, the Belgian artist Henry van de Velde: it emerged quite organically as a response to the work of Vincent van Gogh, to which it was close in time. What in Van Gogh's work was a direct expression of the neuroses of the time, and a prophetic experience of existential anguish and of the menace facing modern Man, in the case of van de Velde was already conceived with the sense of a born architect, putting the material and the means of expression at the service of an idea aimed at a change of reality. Vincent van Gogh's cosmological visions had prepared even the forms which in van de Velde's work became the well-known 'Belgian line' – an endlessly evolving and plastically pulsating curve, which, according to van de Velde, was of expressly psychic origin, for it took strength from whoever drew it. At the same time, van Gogh's visions underlay the entire spiritual endeavour to create a new style which, in a utopian way, was to change reality into a new Paradise.

The instinct towards stylization, found in the most typical works of the period, whose scenery proper was the background of modern cities, paradoxically manifested itself in a cult of Nature. This fascination with Nature, obvious enough not to need close documentation, gave the art of the time the label of 'panbiologism'. It hid its unusual technical aspect to such an extent that retrospective assessment often regarded it as withdrawing from constructive human values and clinging only to the subjective level of our existence. The result is a gap which widened between this art and the endeavours of the avant-garde artists who followed. But it appears today that this judgement, though justifiable as a reaction of the younger generation of artists, was not quite objective. The problem of ornament hides an important counterbalance to the vegetative exuberance of the period style; the requirements of ornamentation led to the naturalistic basis being re-assessed and transmuted into an ingenious graphic system which exceeded the individual uniqueness of the natural phenomenon and objectivized artistic expression into a communicative, socially applicable, visual system. The unconventional genres, e.g. the poster, which this art turned to, did perhaps the greatest service to this aspect of art at the turn of the century. They are today mainly valuable for the vehemence and intensity with which art overcame the traditional differences between major and minor, fine or useful arts, between aesthetic luxury for a small group in society, and rubbish for the rest. Although art around 1900 is often accused of pan-aestheticism, and of following the slogan of 'art for art's sake', it is precisely the posters of the period which show how this art helped to change its age, and with what unusual strength it effectively penetrated to those areas of everyday life normally strongly resistant to the influence of art.

Art at the turn of the 19th and 20th centuries had, of course, its own depth, its own distinctive features. Its mysterious, and, to a certain extent, most profoundly integrating aspect, forms the third, top apex of our triangle, and links up with the period movement that expressed it most fully and deliberately, namely, *Symbolism*.

The literary manifestos of Symbolism were published in the eighties of the last century, and all of them referred to the term '*idea*', which seemed then to have been invalidated by the empirical endeavours of the 'modern age'. Among the Symbolists this concept had no rational meaning, nor was it for them a term of systematic idealist philosophy. They turned to certain of its meanings current, e.g. among the Mannerists of the 16th century,[3] who conceived it metaphysically, yet far more concretely than the later systematic philosophers. In the comparatively loose usage of this term in this period one can distinguish a feeling for the magic and the alchemy of the word. The often-quoted sentences of the poet Stéphane Mallarmé, the initiator and most outstanding figure of mature Symbolism, contain in a nutshell the entire Symbolist view, and, furthermore, express its contribution to modern art: 'To name the object means to suppress three quarters of the enjoyment of a poem, which rests in the happiness of guessing step by step; to suggest it, that is a dream. The perfect application of the secret creates a picture: gradually to evoke an object so as to reveal the mental state or, on the contrary, to choose an object and through a number of solutions to disengage a mental state from it...'[4] The idea here is conceived not only as a thought, but as one in its embryonic state, i.e. as an idea that is revealed in the form of a picture. It is not an aim in itself, but is conceived as an effective means of expression, as the disclosure of the 'mental state' which, at the end of the sublime Symbolist creative process, is to predominate over the initial and 'evoked' object and arises from it as an aura of light. Mallarmé's formulation comprises in ingenious manner the two interlinked aspects of Symbolist treatment of the object. It expresses both Symbolist insight, that is the technique of poetic suggestion and polyvalent meaning, and also that special regard for the artistic material, for the medium of poetic transformation and its own autonomous requirements. Both these aspects then link up in that authentic Symbolism which resists romantic sentimentality and the exaltation of the creator's psychic self, and, in its place, develops a greater sense of the mystery of this world, for its gradual and prudent elaboration. It seeks the revelation of this mystery through intuitive means which can begin to perceive the world in its original substance, in its naturalness and artificiality.

With this concept of intuitive feeling, Symbolism deserves to stand at the apex of our triangle setting the boundaries of art around the year 1900. It gives an inner meaning to the two lower poles of symbolic denotation: naturalistic focusing of attention on the natural object and its visual appearance, and ornamental, decorative elaboration of a system of symbols comprehended as the formal style of the period. The Symbolist 'object' relates to both these poles in equal measure. It unifies their polarity in terms of meaning and forms the basic prerequisite for the domination of content, of the newly conceived and posed idea.

The relationship of these elements forms the basis of what, to this day, attracts us so greatly to the art of this period. In spite of the wide variety of art forms, and in spite of their often brief existence, this art appears as a consistent system. The system was marked not only by period programmes – in the sense of the preceding linking of the apexes of the triangle with Naturalism, Decorative Ornamentalism and Symbolism – it formed a dynamic entity because all its definite elements were mutually complementary, and in their practical application even overlapped, without, in so doing, losing the possibility of being distinguished in period work that often included all of them. Perhaps every important picture of the time can be seen and understood at all three levels of the apexes mentioned – while only their aggregate forms its unmistakable value.

In view of the permanent, internal interchange it is therefore necessary to view our triangle in yet another way:

The inserted shape symbolizes the practical activity of period art striving to implement the programmes of the time and, in transition between them, pushing towards the centre, where we can find the value of concentrated enjoyment for the creator and the spectator. In this centre lies the core of the legacy of art at the turn of the 19th and 20th centuries. Today we are reviving this former enjoyment by approaching it through reconstruction, from the, as it were, petrified apexes of our triangle. It certainly also exists within ourselves. The artists, who are to be the centre of our attention, and their drawings, as intimate personal manifestations, and the drawn theory of art, in this sense open up to us the gates to further understanding.

If, so far, we have dealt with the system of art at the turn of the 19th and 20th centuries, it is now necessary to turn to a discussion of its most outstanding creative personalities in order to maintain a balance between the work created and its creator, so typical of, and important for, modern art. The selection of artists does not set out to be exhaustive. Instead of a general survey we have chosen a given circle which, though far from covering the entire area of contemporary drawing, endeavours to depict some of its basic and most characteristic features.

Alfons Mucha

Alfons Mucha became famous in the nineties, chiefly through his posters for the actress Sarah Bernhardt, the first of which, depicting the famous star in the title-role of Sardou's *Gismonde*, he drew at the very end of 1894. For the next ten years Mucha was among the leading representatives of Parisian *Art Nouveau*. He was one of its founders and, thanks to his quite exceptional draughtsmanship and constant output, became virtually its official graphic artist. Apart from posters, illustrations, decorative panneaux and a variety of different books, he designed jewellery, costumes and sets for the theatre, and even the gigantic Pavilion of Man for the World Exhibition in Paris in 1900. In that decade he proved himself to be a typical personality of the new concept of art which, in contrast to the Impressionists' analysis of the colourful appearance of the world, wished to give it synthesis once again, to unify it and conceive it as a homogeneous entity. This main trend of the period characterizes the whole of Mucha's work. This is as true of the above-mentioned, predominantly style-setting period, which ended with the authoritative pattern-books of pure and applied graphic forms – '*Documents Décoratifs*' (1902) and '*Figures Décoratives*' (1905), as of the later period, in which Mucha's Symbolist ambition to paint large, philosophical and historical pictures and cycles of pictures predominated.

The stylistic value which gave Mucha's work historical significance and brought him into the front rank of the skilful and well-trained draughtsmen crowding the quarters of Paris at the time undoubtedly came into being as an agglomeration of various personal contributions converging in time and crystallizing in certain motifs of form and content, whose typical aggregate came to be distinguished as a new style. In Mucha's case, we must consider all the possible influences, leading to the almost spontaneous birth of a new stylistic attitude which superseded all Mucha's previous work as an academically trained illustrator and designer, who had hitherto exclusively used the established repertoire of forms.

Perhaps the greatest influence on Mucha, among modern painters, was Paul Gauguin, whom Mucha knew from the days before Gauguin's trip in 1891 to the South Seas, and to whom he offered a temporary refuge in his studio in the Rue Grande Chaumière on Gauguin's unexpected return in 1893. He saw Gauguin at work, at first hand.

Though the general tenor of Gauguin's personality may not have suited Mucha, and though he may even have felt a certain professional superiority over Gauguin's self-taught art, Gauguin's work, which he appreciated, must have stirred him to pursue with new courage the search for a solution to the task he had set himself as an artist. Gauguin's views on art, presented with convincing strength, had become accepted by a number of artists of the younger generation, from the Pont Aven group to *Les Nabis*. Paul Gauguin and Vincent van Gogh should be regarded as the true forerunners of modern art, which means that in their work they intuitively foreshadowed modern art as a whole. The artists of the nineties were stimulated by them, not as historic authorities, but through a shared interest, both admiring and critical, in the work of a contemporary, which, nonetheless, showed an unerring sense for authentic period values.

In this manner, Gauguin's work evoked a response in Mucha, who was steeped in Paris art and well versed in the spiritual climate in which this new art was coming into being. He applied and developed these lessons in his own work which did not set out to escape beyond the bounds of European civilization, and did not give in to an idealized, utopian barbarism, as was the case with Gauguin. These differences can be detected in the colour composition of Mucha's posters for Sarah Bernhardt. The colours, apart from the graphic design, immediately attracted the attention of the wider Parisian public. They were striking, since, in contrast to the clamourous tones of the 'street salons' of the time, they combined subdued and tranquil tones, mutually complementary in typical period harmonies of rust, pale-green and violet, so that their general impression was almost one of 'white' posters. They displayed an ingenious harmony of 'flat effect' colours, aspects based on Gauguin's original programme, and, at the same time, in contrast to Gauguin, incomparably greater stress on the line. Mucha's main medium was not colour, however intensive its artificial harmonies were, but drawing, whose flourishing ornamentalism forms the basic structure of all his work.

Stress on drawing corresponds not only to the specific features of Mucha's talent, but, artistically, clearly expresses that important shift in the mission of a work of art where escape from the world of commonplace life is realized not so much by evoking the 'natural' paradise of life on remote and untouched islands, but rather by a blissful immersion into a world of 'more artificial' paradises. Basically, the beautiful naiveté of both attempts, Mucha's and Gauguin's, was identical: to plaster Paris with magnificent posters, and re-shape the entire living environment, or else to show the pride of a prophet pointing elsewhere – both attitudes were based on the same artistic altruism. In the first intention, Mucha and related artists were very nearly successful, if only for a limited period.

The very heart of Mucha's artistic expression, the essence of his work, which can be seen in the languid sensitivity of his heroines, today quite unreproducible, must be sought in the deepest levels of his artistic personality. The spontaneous, yet obsessively repetitive character of his work suggests that we are dealing with something that must have become a fixation during his childhood and early youth. Mucha's greatest experiences as a child, in his native Moravia, were linked with religion, with the mystery of divine service experienced in an aesthetic manner. At a much later age, Mucha recalled in his notes the sensual charm of Catholic services, in which, as a student in Brno, he had participated as a choir singer in the intricacies of Gregorian plain-song. This education, in which music and visual experiences were linked in the child's mind, created the fertile basis of all of Mucha's art, to be easily developed and applied later, when Mucha exchanged the Church for the theatre.

The artistic decoration of the churches themselves must have left a profound impression on the boy. Even if, so far, it is impossible to make a work-to-work comparison, it is nevertheless clear that the innate tone of Mucha's art cannot be understood without considering the special character which Baroque and Rococo had imprinted upon art in the Czech Lands and in Austria by the second half of the 18th century. This art, even now the predominant style in the churches of those countries, was remarkable for the overall effect of its artefacts, carried out in an uncompromisingly emotional manner, and thus suggesting the idea of *Gesamtkunstwerk* shaping the human psyche. This idea reappeared in full strength as the programme of the nineties of the 19th century, often symptomatically linking up with the last of the historical styles of the time, the Neo-Baroque. This may have given rise to the 'Byzantine' quality of Mucha's work, which is referred to in contemporary papers. Their static quality and rich ornamentation is, however, far from stiff – it simply marks the general, representative character of Mucha's works that were meant for the general public. In the baldaquin of their complex ornamental frames there always appears a woman who does not hide her ancestry in the sweet Rococo saints.

Woman was Mucha's main theme. This preoccupation was further accentuated through his cooperation with Sarah Bernhardt, who, according to the taste of the time, seemed the personification of womanhood. Woman was conceived as a symbol, the lively depiction of whom embodied the emotional experience of the mystery of this world. For that reason, the female figure was no academic nude for Mucha, although he did not abandon the skills and idioms of contemporary draughtsmanship. He preferred to make use of them; and this, too, should be regarded as one of the reasons for his social success. Salon painting became popular through drawings, but acquired new value in so doing. While it had formerly given satisfaction only to individual tastes, it now began to express a more general feeling about life. In that sense, the human figure in Mucha's work became integrated through the motif of woman and flower. But not only in the world of nature: for its complex interaction with ornament raised it to the even more attractive sphere of art, of which it became the centre.

Brian Reade has recognized as the basic scheme of Mucha's compositions a shape that recalls the letter Q.[5] It is generally a figure of circular shape formed by the ornamental frame, or even a letter slightly flattened and broadened, recalling a nimbus. Inside it, there is a somewhat asymmetrically placed woman's body, often emphasized by some long and projecting shape spreading the figure, enclosed in a circular form, over the remaining area of the picture. The erotic character of this link is symptomatic and constitutes the effective basis of the entire layout. By this manner of composition Mucha basically overcame the ancient dualism, in which the artistic problem of the relation between figure and ornament disintegrated into a static relationship of ornamental frame and figural inner area. Instead, a new trend, leading to the integration of these two aspects, was here realized. This integration of the pictorial area has a profound meaning: over the entire area there occurs a process of balancing the natural and the abstract form, resulting in a work in which the intense inner pressure of erotic life-giving strength becomes sublimated into a form that was of a socially acceptable, supra-personal character.

Mucha's graphic works possess a special tension, caused by the static posture of his figures and the timeless expression of their faces, contrasted with their stressed contours, which brings life into the picture. The outline of the figure is elaborated in detail by further elements of motif and form, such as flowers and, particularly, the popular, contemporary motif of long, wavy hair. This dynamic motif, corresponding to the drawing of a nude, firmly conceived in the organic structure of the body, is no mere decorative addition. Its very complexity and exuberance suggest that here lies one of the important keys to an understanding of Mucha's entire work.

Mucha's manner of drawing was well described by his son who, though at a later period, frequently observed him at work:

'First he divided the area by outlining the main drawing. Then he at once filled in the empty spaces with shapes; first, only a few, so as to achieve balance, and, then, more and more, which he added simultaneously until the whole drawing was filled with curves and arabesques. He never had a preconceived plan, nor did he concentrate only on one part of the picture. His hand circled confidently across the paper, and each new stroke gave an impulse to another. Sometimes he would play a game with me, in which I was to guess what a certain shape would turn out to be, man, animal or plant? I saw the shapes multiply, but I was unable to make anything of them until, all of a sudden, the mere strengthening of certain outlines, or the link-up of two or three lines, gave rise to a figure in a characteristic pose. It stood out from the flat ornament as in an acrostic, alive, real and yet so intertwined with its setting that I used to be afraid I might lose it again in the tangle of branches or blossoms.'[6]

Of particular interest is the mention of the game, which indicates that Mucha was considering how the spectator would understand the picture, and that he directly counted on his playful participation. The spectator, in other words, was to read the picture in the reverse order to that in which it was created, from the multiplicity and confusion of tiny shapes to the basic forms of the 'main drawing'. This action of the eye was, in reality, to take place more spontaneously, but the very tangle of flowing hair or vegetation, as well as the more abstract ornamental shapes, basically led the spectator's eye along until the meaning of the drawing, together with the theme of its subject, became clear to him. All this complex graphic game was, however, not to lead merely to the solution of an artistic rebus – its chief delight obviously rested in the enjoyment of the constant metamorphosis of shapes, in the inner life of the drawing, which thus acquired a more profound artistic value. This approach by Mucha to his drawings is basically a modern one and, though cloaked in an historically unique period garb, it foreshadowed techniques which are often considered to have been the achievement of the later avant-garde artists.

It can, moreover, be said that the overall conception of a drawing as an artistic and psychic event develops the 'archetypal' picture which is frequently recognized as one of the main motifs of all modern art. Mucha, in his linearism and ornamentalism, in fact, interprets the pictorial area as a labyrinth. But these pictorial labyrinths are not merely schematic neolithic spirals and meanders. They are more 'modern', for they do not eliminate the element of chance from the symbol. They include the moment of graphic spontaneity and automatism, as well as illusive fragments of naturalistic shapes. This is, clearly, where the roots of Mucha's graphic form lay. His line, which is most strikingly employed in such details as snake-like braids of hair, or spreading tendrils of floral vegetation, tends, like every line in mature Art Nouveau, to be continuous, infinite. It is a continuity of forms, long sectors and minor accumulations, constantly uncoiling or winding, through which the spectator's eye wanders without ever getting completely lost, because he is never left entirely to himself. In the end, he is always guided, even if in an unobtrusive manner. Of similar kind are the concentric shapes appearing as nimbi behind the heads of Mucha's figures, or applied even in pure ornamental structures, e.g. on Mucha's carpet designs, which, like ancient mosaics, or Druidic stone structures, were intended to cover places of social 'initiation', namely, the civil salons. The geometrical symbolism of Mucha's concentric shapes shows even more convincingly how much the artist was obsessed with this theme. They always have some kind of firmer edge, which sometimes turns into a symbol of the horseshoe, or of the lunar crescent. Inside, there is a field filled with an intricate configuration of smaller shapes, which, however, always have their own, asymmetrically placed focal point. Usually, this is the face of the figure. The spectator's eye, which, at first, might be attracted only by a certain frivolous detail of the drawing, is irresistibly led further and further into the maze of the ornamental system, into the main concentric structure and from there out again, often to some concrete attribute, which the poster, for example, was to draw attention to.

The fact that Mucha did not hesitate to apply the total principle even in 'bread-and-butter' commissions seems to support the opinion that the whole system, and particularly its significance, was created and conceived entirely intuitively, which would increase its historic, symptomatic significance. It corresponds well to Mucha's interests outside the arts, of which we have precise information, for instance, his interest in Spiritualism.[7] The experiments with a medium, carried out in the company of the astronomer Flammarion and the librarian de Rochas, may well have had a direct influence on his art, because they were aimed at expressing the spiritual content of the medium's gestures. In this sense, all Mucha's figures should be understood as spiritualistic media of a kind, as an intermediary link of communication with the Other World. Thus, his occultism led into the labyrinth, because the latter always appeared as a picture of the Realm of the Dead. But, in his art, the dominating feature of these relations is not morbidity, because in his work one passes through the labyrinth of forms in just the same way as the Spiritualists pass through death. The aim is not to wander in shadows, but to attain a new reality, a new certainty. The infinity of this relationship, expressed artistically as the 'infinity' of the *Art Nouveau* line, is, in fact, synonymous with immortality.

This interpretation is, indeed, a later one. It was not an a priori programme, as can be shown by Mucha's drawings. Apart from the work shown to the public we can find drawings quite large in size, executed in charcoal and coloured chalks, which point to the other side of his personality. With their dark tones, out of which seem to flare up only sparks of bright colours, they seem to arise out of the psychic depths of Mucha's labyrinth, out of its dark realm. In theme, too, they are rather gloomy – scenes of blind wanderings and of cul-de-sacs. The drawing called 'Absinthe' seems, at first sight, remote from the rest of Mucha's works in its drastic expression. But it is proof of the authenticity of Mucha's art, proof of his own descent into the depths of the labyrinth, proof that his seemingly ephemeral art, taken only as a work of fashion, is based on a more profound experience of life, over which his style spreads like an enigma, 'artistic' in the original sense of that word.

1.

Alfons Mucha:
Invitation to
a Banquet
1898, Indian ink,
56.5 × 40 cm
K 12393 National
Gallery, Prague

Alfons Mucha:
Profile of a Woman
with Peacock
Feather in
a Decorative Frame
*1899, pencil and
watercolour,
80 × 30 cm
K 29308 National
Gallery, Prague*

3

Alfons Mucha:
Profile of a Woman
with Orchids in
a Decorative Frame
1899, pencil and
watercolour,
80 × 30 cm
K 29309 National
Gallery, Prague

Alfons Mucha:
Job
poster design, 1896,
Indian ink and
watercolour,
120 × 44 cm
K 30505 National
Gallery, Prague

6.

Alfons Mucha:
Exhibition of
Architecture and
Engineering
poster design, 1897,
charcoal and
watercolour,
108.5 × 85 cm
K 9461 National
Gallery, Prague

Alfons Mucha:
Woman Sitting
in an Armchair
sketch for a poster,
pencil and
watercolour,
49.5 × 44 cm
K 30410 National
Gallery, Prague

Alfons Mucha:
Nude Wandering
in the Evening
Landscape
*charcoal and coloured
chalks, 47 × 62 cm
K 31622 National
Gallery, Prague*

9.

Alfons Mucha:
Absinthe
*charcoal and coloured
chalks, 48 × 62 cm
K 31626 National
Gallery, Prague*

Alfons Mucha:
Woman with Lilies
c. 1902, charcoal,
123 × 45.4 cm
K 30500 National
Gallery, Prague

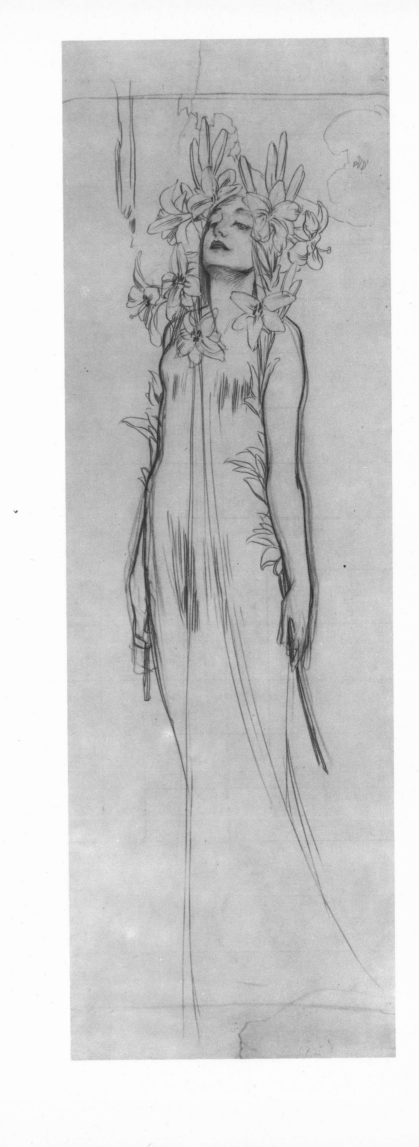

Aubrey Beardsley

Beardsley's art matured within the brief span of only seven years before his death from tuberculosis. Yet in this relatively short period there arose such a distinctive and inimitable collection of sets of illustrations, individual drawings for journals and occasional drawings, that today Beardsley can be seen not only as one of the most outstanding figures of art at the end of the 19th century, but also as an artist, whose work foreshadowed some of the general aspects of modern art.

Disregarding the unfavourable circumstance of his too sudden fame, and equally sudden oblivion, the historic value of Beardsley's work can be better understood when we realize that he was the almost logical culmination of a development that took place in English art throughout the 19th century. His work, exceptional at first sight, fits smoothly into the pattern of English culture, and forms the climax especially of those trends that were not officially acknowledged. It is impossible to imagine Beardsley without William Blake, without the Pre-Raphaelites and, in particular, without E. Burne-Jones, whom he followed consciously; even without William Morris and his movement, supported by John Ruskin, though Morris himself voiced certain objections to Beardsley's work. Beardsley based his very first drawings on the work of one of the pioneers of the English movement for the renewal of the arts, particularly of decorative art, and their new status in the life of society, Kate Greenaway. While the artistic genesis of Beardsley's graphic style is quite clearly seen, there do exist differences, arising chiefly from the inner feelings and content of Beardsley's works.

Beardsley appears as a 'Decadent', in opposition to the deeply-rooted moralism and sentimental idealism of recent English tradition. In his work, the undercurrents of the Romantic world outlook came to the fore again, opposing social Utopianism and the gospel of Christian love and innocence, and crystallized in a special and urgent form. He liked to ridicule, to be ironic; and this disrespect for ideals was more than an occasional occurrence. Beardsley was fatefully attracted by negation.

These attitudes were fostered by the cultural refinement typical of the spiritual climate of England in the nineties. The 'aesthetic movement', best represented by the poet and dramatist Oscar Wilde, and based mainly on literature, found commensurate expression in the fine arts. Beardsley's predecessor was the American painter James McNeill Whistler, who had lived in Paris and was well acquainted with French culture. His 'Peacock Room', made for Lord Leyland in London in the years 1876–77, influenced the young Beardsley directly, and did so both through its overall atmosphere of exceptional elegance and luxury, and through its individual motifs, such as the ingeniously coloured 'white' portrait of the woman dominating the room. Particularly influential was the unusually pure graphic treatment of the motif of the peacocks with their magnificent tails painted on the insides of the shutters. Whistler was a direct forerunner of Beardsley, with his dandyism, satirical wit and feeling for the extraordinary, and for the shocking, almost exotic, matter-of-factness with which he introduced to England a new cult of Oriental, particularly Japanese, art. The only difference between them was that between a painter exercising his imagination with restrained colours, and a draughtsman expressing himself in black and white.

This affinity to all his predecessors can be quite concretely traced in the first two of Beardsley's large commissions for illustrations. The first set, which was to accompany Sir Thomas Malory's 'Morte D'Arthur', came to include 350 drawings, and freed him in 1892 from all need for employment, enabling him to devote himself exclusively to the arts, in which he was, in fact, self-taught. Beardsley's starting point here was the idea of illustrating modern books, as put forward by William Morris, but gradually he abandoned the original terms of that idea, turning to freely-conceived medieval patterns reproduced in wood-engravings.

It is interesting, in view of the subsequent development of his work, to note that here Beardsley devoted a two-page illustration to a scene in which the devil in female form appears to Sir Bors, one of the heroes, and tempts him. This theme proved so attractive to Beardsley that it came to dominate all his subsequent work.

The second commission established Beardsley's fame and has kept it alive to this day. He was asked to illustrate an edition of Oscar Wilde's play 'Salome', translated into English from its French original. The book, with Beardsley's original binding decorated with the 'coat-of-arms' motif of peacock's eyes, was published in 1894. Beardsley was given the task on the strength of a drawing he had made the year before, which, with unmistakable intuition, encompassed the very substance of Wilde's play, precisely expressing the spirit of the time. Mario Praz, in his study of 'Black Romanticism' of the 19th century described that special affinity which the culture of the second half of the 19th century felt for the theme of Salome.[8] In Symbolist art, a great influence was exerted by the French painter Gustave Moreau, whose paintings, 'Salomé' and 'Apparition', exhibited in 1876, greatly stirred French literary circles at the end of the century, particularly J. K. Huysmans, who mentioned them in his famous novel 'A Rebours'. The development of this theme reached its climax in the work of Oscar Wilde. In earlier versions of the story of the death of St. John the Baptist, Salome had appeared as a secondary character, the mere tool of evil and personal revenge. But now she had become the central figure. Her transformation was seen dramatically in the scene which Beardsley drew in his first drawing, where Salome kisses the severed head of the Christian martyr, with an excited pleasure, symbolical of her perversity.

Beardsley in his illustrations even further intensified Wilde's image of Salome as a female type of this period when presenting her in a highly unconventional manner, often diverting from the pattern, in various situations. This includes 'Salome's Toilet', which shows this deliberate trend in Beardsley's work most clearly and points expressly to the sources of his ideas. For on the bookshelf of this Salome can be seen a volume of the 'divine' Marquis de Sade, whom Praz proclaimed the Grey Eminence of this 'second' Romanticism.

But Beardsley's art contains much more than can be explained by simply referring to these influences and sources. He was a creator who, above all, gave pronounced, modern form to themes which until that time were often clothed in mythological historicism. He created a truly living, visual type, the axis unifying all his work, and his graphic style was quite exceptionally effective.

Beardsley's graphic form of expression was one of the first calls for a major simplification of artistic expression, for rendering it down to its elements. Using just black and white, Beardsley, with the aid of lines and surfaces, achieved an unforgettably effective graphic pattern. The striving for perfection, often considered a typical feature of Beardsley's work, led him to a stage where he did not do extensive preparatory work for his final drawings in which he undoubtedly broke with academic tradition. He would do one drawing over and over again until he achieved what might be called the principle of inner necessity, something that corresponded precisely to his feeling and demand for 'correct form'. That was a value vital to the general purport of Beardsley's work. The animality of Beardsley's women, culminating in his Messalinas as representing insuppressible instinctiveness, is always balanced by great artistry and ideal elegance of form. This special compound of two, basically contradictory, trends creates the inner tension in Beardsley's work. It is clearly that element of his drawings that is so exceptionally attractive to our own days.

It is interesting that this value has its roots in Beardsley's concept of the picture, in his manner of work with black and white, and his treatment of the line and area. Beardsley, doubtless through Whistler, had imbibed the lesson of Japanese art, particularly Japanese woodcuts, greatly admired by all European modern artists. One of the likenesses of Salome, after all, clings so closely to Japanese pattern as to be almost a caricature. One can find in Beardsley's work a whole series of motifs and subjects taken directly from Japanese art. And it was Beardsley who drew perhaps the most consistent lesson from this style, and embodied it in the bases of modern European graphic art. Like the Japanese he abandoned shadow and, therewith, the three-dimensional depiction of his figures and objects. In this way, he parted company with the typical European concept of contours and with that basic contradiction between object and space, which, in the Renaissance, formed the basis of perspective depiction in European art. By abandoning this classical concept of space he could then consistently approach the picture as a graphic pattern, with its starting point not in the details, but in its totality. This new, total, concept was then enlivened from within by being treated as the mutual inter-relationship of white and black, balancing over the area. Through this new contradiction the old one of figure versus background was eliminated. Only much later did German *Gestalt* psychology come to comprehend these relationships as those of basic shapes. In the work of Beardsley there came into being, basically intuitively and in a 'pure' artistic embodiment, a new concept of unity and totality, which has even some philosophical meaning, and which forms the substantial contribution that Beardsley has made towards the establishment of modern art.

It should be stressed that the character of this conception was not one of purely rational consideration; it arose from, and was realized in, the living process of creation. In this sense, the Symbolist and Decadent *univers discours* which Beardsley experienced so fully and absolutely, rose again to the fore. His orchestration of white and black was not founded on rational calculation, but on intuitive harmonization, giving the basic impression of constant balancing, mobility of the whole structure, and even an impression that individual areas might possibly be interchanged. The significant places, where black encounters white, form long lines which, again, are not drawn in the traditional sense, but seem to divide the area. At the same time, this division is sensitive to the stressed detail. It might be said that Beardsley felt the area to be a total field of force on which two elements – expressed in black and white – meet; and their battle is crystallized into the firmer state of symbols and attributes. His style, of course, was not expressionistically 'immediate', but a special value was here undeniably given by a certain restraint, and even irony, by his wish to suggest meaning and emphasize the exhibitionism of the entire action. This tone of expression was undoubtedly firmly linked with the specific core of Beardsley's attitude to life. If the question of Beardsley's homosexuality, which suggests itself here, is adduced (for which there does not, however, seem to be clear enough proof) one must recall that Beardsley was simply expressing, with great intensity, a certain cultural idiom, which was characteristic of a distinct current in the whole of English culture during the 19th century.[9]

Only in this connection can one understand the immense reaction to Oscar Wilde's trial in the year 1895, which, undeservedly, was also of serious consequence for Beardsley. This event, important both culturally, and, in a sense, politically, in which the forces of order reacted strongly to an intellectual's provocation, inevitably further upset the already unstable place of the Decadents in society and was bound to cause a crisis among them. In their growing isolation they turned away from the present. Indeed, in the work of Beardsley one can detect a traditionalism from that date on, which took the form of escape into the safer spheres of historicism. In the morphology of Beardsley's later work we can find many references to Rococo, Neo-classicism and 16th century Mannerism. It was some of these aspects that his imitators enthusiastically adopted. But in the work of Beardsley himself there was no break in continuity.

If we regard his work as a whole, it becomes clear that it does not deny tradition. Beardsley, on the contrary, is syncretic. But the uniqueness of his achievement lies in his having absorbed tradition in an unerringly clear way. In its immense variety, amassed by the historicism of the 19th century, he revealed its parameters, and thus renewed the basic significance of culture. Culture, in its visual, artistic and pictorial aspects, ceased to be simply a store of good taste, and once again became a tool to disturb the spectator. This encounter between Beardsley and those who held the same views, and the accepted customs of conventional English society, is proof that their new culture was understood and assessed in such a way.

The decadent and hyper-erotic, at times almost obscene, features of Beardsley's art were meant, in the first place, to shock. Their tone was, at the same time, one of burlesque. They demolished with irony the basic assumptions of poetic and historical fiction, and in this constant encounter of the irrelevant and the relevant, or the comic and the tragic, which the writer Arthur Koestler has said is the basis of all humour, they formed an effective structure of expression.[10] In the case of Beardsley, however, it was not merely occasional, it was inwardly inevitable.

Beneath the cloak of exhibitionism in Beardsley's work, with increasing urgency and concentration, arose profound and dark forces. Beardsley clearly perceived this force in Wagner's music, to the themes of which he devoted a series of drawings which are among his most outstanding. This power seemed ever more irrepressibly to break up the fragile strands of decorative preciosity which served only as a necessary contrast and a sophisticated complement to the basic and timeless eroticism of his imagination. The melancholy of Beardsley's last works, in which the contrast of black and white is supplemented with the technique of washing, by using half-shades like the old sfumato, can properly be explained in terms of the incapacitating illness that was leading to its inexorable end. His belated conversion to Catholicism might, superficially, be explained as 'acquiring wisdom'. But in the large, sweetly seductive eyes of the last pictures of women, placed as if at the end of the 18th century in a strange, timeless vacuum, their torpid calm foretelling the oncoming storm, the themes of all of Beardsley's work reached their consummation.

If Beardsley's Salome were to be regarded in the light of the meaning attributed to this motif by Symbolism in the second half of the 19th century, she might be taken as a modern embodiment of evil, as a demoniacally beautiful witch, who is 'enamoured of evil in the form of perverse and diabolical temptation' (G. Moreau). The knightly ideal that was still present in the story of 'Morte D'Arthur' faded away in Beardsley's work, and its first historical, but in Beardsley's work, the last representative, St. John the Baptist, is beheaded. It is a matter of subtle metaphors, rather than the direct victory of evil. The symbolic murder which Beardsley presented in the story of Salome meant a descent from asceticism to vitalism, a retreat which was achieved by a sudden reversal. At the same time this reversible, metamorphic value, inherent in Beardsley's technique of draughtsmanship, hints at a new harmony of elemental contradictions, presented in a most dramatic and dynamic relationship.

Aubrey Beardsley:
Poster for
'The Spinster's Scrip'
1895, Indian ink,
36.2 × 23.6 cm
Beardsley Collection
41 Princeton University
Library, Princeton

Aubrey Beardsley:
Salome's Toilet
1894, Indian ink,
22.3 × 15.9 cm
British Museum,
London

Aubrey Beardsley:
The Wagnerites
Indian ink and white,
20.6 × 17.8 cm
Victoria and Albert
Museum, London

Aubrey Beardsley:
Siegfried Act II
washed Indian ink,
40 × 28.5 cm
Victoria and Albert
Museum, London

Aubrey Beardsley:
The Peacock Skirt
1894, Indian ink,
22.5 × 15.8 cm
Fogg Art Museum,
Harvard University,
Massachusetts

Aubrey Beardsley:
J'ai baisé ta bouche,
Iokanaan
1893, Indian ink and
watercolour,
27.7 × 14.7 cm
Beardsley Collection
97 Princeton University
Library, Princeton

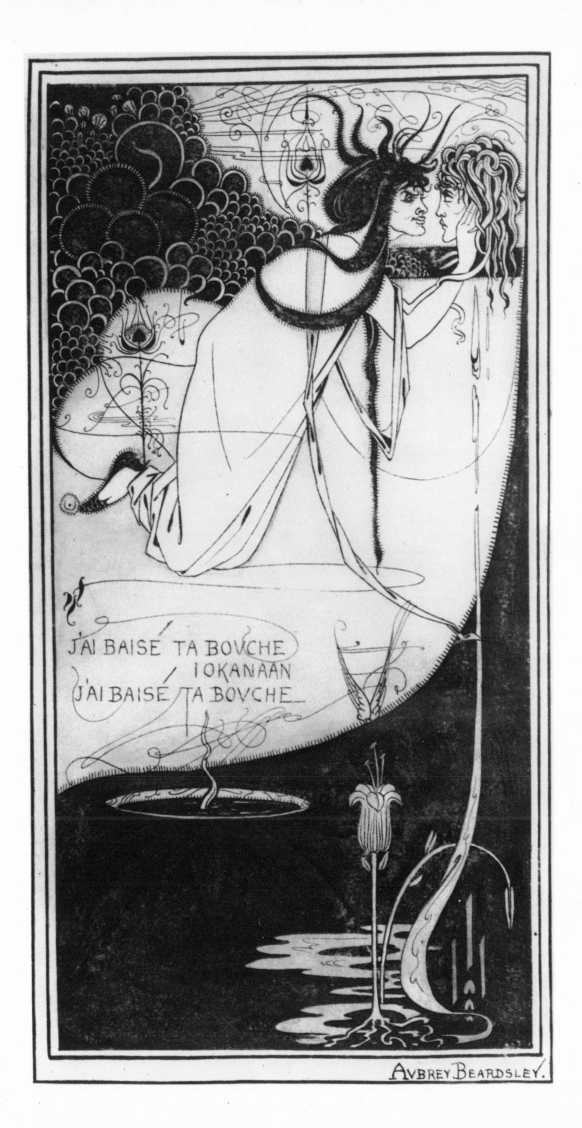

Aubrey Beardsley:
Erda
1896, Indian ink,
13.8 × 8.8 cm
British Museum,
London

Odilon Redon

Mucha and Beardsley were graphic artists who worked in the nineties, when the atmosphere was propitious for new concepts, and new modern views were meeting with response among a wider public. At that time, as the example of these two artists shows, the prime task facing the artist was that of employing the interaction between the creator and society to create a new style. It was solved in various ways. In the case of Mucha, considerable adaptation was achieved, while, with Beardsley, the reverse side of such a relationship, which at core was one of conflict, was stressed. Both cases, however, presupposed an inner preparation for harmonization which would create spiritual prerequisites for them, both historically and as individual harbingers of the developing spiritual situation.

Another such pioneer was Odilon Redon. His original work reached full development in the eighties. Even though, until the end of the century, his work was in black and white – his famous 'Noirs', or charcoal drawings and lithographs – and colour appeared only in the final years of the 19th century, Redon was, nevertheless, one of the leading personalities in artistic development at this period and might even be considered a model for artists of the Symbolist movement.

Redon was born in the year 1840, and like his contemporary, the sculptor Auguste Rodin, suffered a great deal of hardship before he achieved recognition. His attempts to become an academic painter ended in fiasco. His brief period in the studio of the painter Gerome at the École des Beaux-Arts ended abruptly, since their attitudes to depicting the model, and their general views on art, were fundamentally in conflict. Later, Redon wrote that the Professor wanted him to draw form with a firm outline, while he saw it vibrating. Instead of the required overall simplification of vision in the students' imitative works, Redon demanded his basic right as a creative artist to be original, to use, without restriction, whatever means he needed, including traditional modes, in the interpretation of reality.

Redon's consequent isolation changed only in the middle of the eighties, when the representatives of modern art began to meet and talk together and form groups. Yet the substance of Redon's art developed during his involuntary isolation in the decade that preceded his meeting with Gauguin and his success at the Brussels Salon of the Twenty.

The first set of works typical of Redon was an album of lithographs entitled 'In a Dream', published in 1879. In 1881 for the first time he exhibited his charcoal drawings, in the premises of the editorial office of the magazine Vie Moderne. Even though they did not rouse wide response, J. K. Huysmans, the writer, went to see the exhibition. Huysmans at once recognized in Redon a kindred spirit, and, in his seminal novel 'A Rebours' cited the work of the almost unknown artist among the authentic voices of the new 'Decadent' taste. Huysmans wrote: 'These drawings simply were out of this world. Most of them transcended the borderlines of painting, and opened the way to quite a special kind of the fantastic, having its origins in the pathological, and in delirium'.

Redon later objected to the manner in which Huysmans regarded his art. If we consider his work in its entirety, including his colour pictures, we can hardly agree that, ultimately, the source of this rich, poetical inspiration lay in something decadent and monstrous. On the other hand, however, a gifted and sensitive beholder such as Huysmans, seeking to point out the unusual aspects of Redon's work, was able to spot the strange, expressive quality of Redon's black and white fantasies, a strangeness which sprang not only from the bizarre, dream-like and mysterious subjects of the drawings, but came unequivocally from them as a clear and direct expression of a severely depressing, and even dangerous, mental situation.

The intensity of this feeling of deep and inner fear is demonstrated by the repetition in the broad range of Redon's visions of certain basic motifs appearing in various forms round his simple geometrical figures, and recurring like an obsession. In Redon's first set of lithographs, 'In a Dream', the motif of a rotating, flying or loosely reposing globe, often anthropomorphized as a human head, appeared several times. Such fantastic globe-heads appear in Redon's work in a great variety of forms: as a head with small wings flying above the vast ocean, on which there cruises a barge with a triangular sail; as a head forming the fruit of a strange plant which grows out of the swamp; as the severed head of a martyr resting on a dish; as a skull; as a flood of tiny heads – balloons receding into the deep black of Redon's imaginary universe. At times, this motif is even zoomorphized with quite exceptional effect, as in the case of Redon's spiders, one of which has a devilish smile, while another is weeping. Mostly, however, these shapes are not enlivened with an expressive shock. On the contrary, they are isolated or separated as fragments, being sealed within themselves, as on the beautiful print 'Head of Orpheus Floating on the Waters' – which might well serve as a general symbol of Redon's art – where the closed eyes of the forefather of poets suggest the theme of inner vision, a theme central to Symbolism, and where the tragic and acquiescent aspects of the Orphean theme have been emphasized.

In the silence of Redon's primordial space, the expressions of these heads stiffen into the form of masks, in whose immobility the chief impact is that of the hypnotically-fixed, black eyes. This whole motif culminates and concentrates its expression in the eye. From the print 'Vision' (1879), where the motif of the eye occurs as the miraculous vision of an immense eye-ball, appearing in a mighty colonnade to a wonder-struck human pair, this theme was transmuted in other drawings as an immense eye floating like a balloon in non-illusive, weightless space. How attractive these forms were for Redon can be gathered from the fact that they often appeared in flat form as clock faces and mysterious, astronomical clocks counting out the hours of Fate, or as discs, or black cosmic suns.

The origin of these motifs in the works of Redon has already been traced in the course of art-historical comparison, and its relation to Gustave Moreau's picture 'Apparition', where Salome has a vision of the severed head of St. John the Baptist in a miraculous halo, has been shown.[11] Since a drawing by Redon on that theme, done about 1878, is known, there is no doubt of the influence. At the same time, it is interesting to realize that, in Redon's work, the role of Salome is entirely neutralized, while the head, with a typically melancholic expression, appears in the company of another spherical object, spontaneously, as it were, without any clear reason in the story. Furthermore, a lithograph by I. I. Grandville from the year 1844 has been found, which shows, satirically, a crowd of men, their heads changed into one big eye, gaping at a bust of a romantically languid beauty. Even this comparison might be considered legitimate, mainly in the sense that the link here is a fixed ideal image, transposed in Grandville's work to a humourous and comic level, while Redon used it almost metaphysically.

At the same time, it is clear that these associations alone cannot explain why Redon was so drawn to these motifs, nor what constituted their deeper meaning for him. This can only be discovered by considering them in relation to the psychology of the artist, which would, of course, have pre-determined Redon to select precisely those examples from preceding tradition which would directly stimulate the development of his own imagination.

The common 'denominator' of all Redon's motifs is clearly the circle, a simple geometrical figure. The circular form serves as a basis, not in a 'purely' artistic sense, but in regard to meaning. So, it varies in different ways and can be anthropomorphized into a human head, or contaminated with the form of an ellipse, which again is primarily of importance in respect of meaning. In this sense, the circle is an intuitive manifestation of the artist's claim to the universal character of his work. It is, indeed, a symbol of the whole world and its situation. Redon, believing that art should 'suggest', strongly intensifies the evocation of emotion by putting man in a strange, fantastic non-space, beyond the framework of current probability.

In his 'Noirs', however, Redon's world of symbolism swarms with demons. This entire set by Redon is 'demonological'. His demons are not, however, free of his obsession with spherical form. Their bodies are vague. The main thing once again are the heads, emerging out of an incomprehensible, dream-like setting, and in them, again, immense eyes in the centre, as dark as bottomless wells. The outer stiffness of Redon's scenes is well compensated by their inner mobility, which, mainly later and especially in the sets towards the end of that epoch, such as 'The Temptation of St. Anthony', or 'The Apocalypse', exploded into dynamic tones using sharp contrasts of black and white. By the disintegration, or re-constitution, of circular clusters of forms, there arose a sort of radiation – an effusion of psychic energy itself.

These considerations take us to the very core of Redon's achievement. His vision is a personal one, and cannot be called literary, since the most important questions were dealt with on his own artistic plane. Here, the otherwise inexplicable super-pressures of Redon's fantasy acquired sense, and the authenticity of his testimony, both personal and of broader social and historic value, became established. Above all, his starting symbol is the eye, as an explicitly artistic attribute, as the basic reminder that we are truly dealing with a vision; a vision of the 'Other World', as Redon expressed it in his controversy with contemporary, 'retinal' painting.

It should be remembered that, artistically speaking, all these values were only just coming into being. 'Suggestive art is something like the emanation of an object in a dream, in which thinking comes to an end. Decadence or not, that's what it is. I would prefer to say it is growth...' wrote Redon in 1894. Such psychic growth is, of course, not without pitfalls and dangers. Its overtness and value is achieved in the face of a great risk. This inturned quality, this conception of art as a direct expression of a major battle in the artist's mind, and its central place in his personality, is expressed in a variation on a beautiful drawing from the year 1887, 'The Drowned' or 'Dream Culminates in Death', intended as an accompaniment to the solemn reading of Edmond Picard's monodrama, 'Juré'. The head of the bearded man, resembling Redon himself, is drifting on the dark surface of the Stygian waters. In one drawing it absorbs, with eyes closed, the radiation of the black sun dominating the entire dark, primordial space; elsewhere it gapes at the skeleton which, with an ironic grin, empty eyeholes turned towards the beholder, is approaching the drowned man in a cloud of light. The traditional symbolism of light is inverted here because the sun is black – it is meant to be the black sun of melancholy – while the light issues from the skeleton, from death. Lautréamont inverted the traditional values in like manner. In Redon's work it is not, therefore, a matter of the fixed, traditional antithesis between light and dark, but of what he called 'growth'. Black occupies a specific place within the range of Redon's Symbolist metaphors. He wrote that it was the most important colour, that it derives its vitality from the mysterious sources of health. It was vital, and it reflected basic Substance. Again, in 1913, Redon wrote that it was not pleasing, that it did not rouse sensuality and was therefore an envoy of the spirit. Black, in other words, did not, in terms of simple idealistic opposition, represent dull matter as opposed to the light of the spirit, but it was in itself the highest concentration of the basic primordial matter, out of which grows spirituality. The much-admired deep black of Redon's charcoals and lithographs has this meaningful background.

In this respect, inner continuity appears to be very important for the whole status of Redon's work. This applies even to the spherical forms. Moreover, it seems that Redon derived prime satisfaction from the very act of applying black to the surface. It is of a linear and kinetic character, and from it derives the link of black and creative strength by means of the line, about which Redon wrote that it was a force emerging from the depths and pointing directly to the spiritual. This is, in fact, similar to Henry van de Velde, who in a well-known statement declared that the line took its strength from whoever drew it. This suggests that all artistic means were here conceived as eminently meaningful, that they corresponded directly to the psyche, and to its processes of expression.

We can notice movement and development in the continuity of Redon's work. The demonology of Redon's charcoals and lithographs is, after all, also 'black' in the traditional sense, since the circle here expresses even the feeling of threat. Some of Redon's demons do not lack a certain degree of aggressiveness, e.g. 'Lonely Juggler', and others. A frequent theme of these works is the struggle against anxiety. Its source has been revealed in the specific circumstances of Redon's childhood. He grew up, separated from his parents, in a lonely house, Peyrelebade, perched next to the ocean. His introversion intensified by this setting, Redon came finally to like this environment so much that he returned there for his holidays until the year 1897, when the house had to be put up for sale. It is clearly important that it was there that he drew his black charcoals, which he turned into lithographs in Paris in the winter season, and that the loss of Peyrelebade meant, in fact, the end of Redon's 'Noirs'. It may well have been that, during his subsequent stays, he experienced again some traumatic shock that he may have suffered there in childhood. On the other hand, there can be little doubt that the 'demonology' came out in Redon's work only after the middle of the seventies, while the earlier drawings and sketches from Peyrelebade and its surroundings do not differ from the landscape views of the Barbizons, whom Redon admired at the time. Redon's authentic form of expression was obviously born under the pressure of the need for self-realization as he grew older. This does not exclude it from being a re-activation of some psychic experience in childhood, which somehow fitted in with the stress situation of the adult Redon, who, as an artist, was unable to find his place among the French artists of the seventies. Redon's entire psychic material acquired meaning only in the world of art, as an artistic projection, and thus became the stimulus for his creative work.

Redon's obsession with circular forms, disguised as physiognomic and objective-fantastic symbols, might, in this respect, be characterized as a circular neurosis, as an expressive tension closely linking the psychic situation of Redon the man with the world of objectivized art forms which Redon encompassed as an artist. In this connection he wrote: 'Nature orders us to use the gifts it has lent us. Mine led me to the world of dreams; the torture of fantasy and surprise which appeared to me under my working instruments I let pass over, but I also guided them and bent them to the laws of art that I know, that I feel. All in order to kindle in the spectator that vagueness lying at the remote end of thinking in the full strength of its attraction and spontaneous charm.'[12]

This trend towards circular forms, which is seen everywhere in Redon's 'Noirs', was an expression of his longing and striving to achieve totality, adjustment to the world and harmony as a human being. That this endeavour was not something invented, forced upon him, is proved by Redon's stress on the concreteness of his work. In this connection, special meaning should be attached to the often quoted remark that he felt the oncome of a spiritual spasm only when he was copying, as neatly as possible, a piece of flint, a blade of grass, a hand or a profile, and that he then had to create and depict all he saw in his fantasy; or to another famous statement, to the effect that he placed the logic of the visible at the service of the invisible. It should be realized that these are all natural objects which can also be seen as shapes approaching, if not circular form, then integral outline. The grass, like the trees, represents here the natural dynamic aspect of the overall idea of art as 'growth', which, in the case of trees, is, in fact, a fairly common symbolism.

Although Redon's conception of art is, at first sight, so extraordinary, it is remarkable that it quite organically linked up all the three elementary aspects that give rise to a work of art. In 1887, Redon wrote that a work of art arose from three sources: tradition, reality of nature and personal inventiveness. By this dynamically-conceived triangle he seems to have expressed a new ideal and a new proposition for all modern art. At the core of artistic work is creativeness, responsive to the world, renewing and uplifting in fundamental harmony the world of human values.

In the concluding years of the 19th century colour returned to Redon's work. K. Berger has pointed out that there is no contradiction between the period of 'Noirs' and the colour symphonies created in the subsequent two decades; but a connection, evinced by the fact that Redon's late graphic cycles came close to paintings in character, and particularly by the increasingly important light effects, beginning with the remarkable print 'Profile of Light' from the year 1886.[13] Redon's light, bearer of a spiritual emanation, did not enter the picture from outside, it was literally born from the deep velvet of Redon's black. His colour, too, in the pastels and in the later oil paintings, had a specific quality of light, which appears as coloured light. The development of colour effects occurred in Redon's work as he lit up the entire area of the picture, as he abandoned the intense black shades, or rather brought about their active transformation. And, indeed, the majority of pictures of this late period show flowers.

The proposition that Redon's work displays an innate continuity can equally be upheld by arguments from psychology. His circular neurosis reached its climax in this late period and was cured. In his later charcoal drawings and sets of lithographs the circular forms were strikingly emphasized. The theme of the radiation from fantastic heads, which are linked with the motifs of a mighty tree or shine like fiery bodies from space, was repeated over and over again. It is not far from balloons to flowers, yet the basic tonality and meaning of the story has changed. The former isolated, fragmentary, and melancholic circular forms are now opened up as flowers, forming a new entity as mysterious, brilliantly-coloured bunches of flowers in a vase. The vase is now a new circular form but, by allusion to the former symbolism of concave female forms, it suggests a container of life. Further possibilities of how to give these circular forms a novel content appear. For example, Redon painted a transparent, lit-up rose window in the 'Cathedral', and magnificent shells, inside which there appeared a female form, in 'The Birth of Venus' (1912). All these shapes can be considered non-orthodox manifestations of Jung's 'mandalas', forms built around a centre, which are deeply symptomatic expressions of a psychic situation. The happy final period in Redon's life and art coincided with an increased interest in religion, particularly in Christianity and Buddhism. This interest was, of course, not intense, and simply reflected the situation resulting from the favourable growth of the artist's powers. His true sustaining force, which led him to the liberated colour visions of his last works, was art. And, about this, Redon wrote from his own experiences: 'Art is the highest force, mighty, healing and hallowing – it opens up like a flower.'

19.

Odilon Redon:
Laughing Spider
1881, charcoal,
49.5 × 39 cm
RF 29932 Cabinet des
Dessins du Musée du
Louvre, Paris

20

Odilon Redon:
La Fleur de marécage
charcoal, 49 × 33 cm
651 Rijksmuseum
Kröller-Müller,
Otterlo

21.

Odilon Redon:
Head of Orpheus
Floating on the Waters
1881, charcoal,
41 × 34 cm
648 Rijksmuseum
Kröller-Müller,
Otterlo

Odilon Redon:
The Drowned
(Dream Culminates
in Death)
1887, charcoal,
54 × 36.5 cm
52398 Prentenkabinet,
Rijksmuseum,
Amsterdam

Odilon Redon:
The Birth of Venus
1912, pastel,
83 × 64 cm
1220 Musée du Petit
Palais, Paris

24.

Edvard Munch

Art in the nineties of the last century found in Edvard Munch a supreme representative of that personal intensity that forged a close link between artistic expression and the imaginary and emotional world of the artist. In this respect Munch is a typical representative of a new artistic individualism, which largely ignored conventions, and proceeded with steadfast dedication, whatever the consequences might be, to trace and express certain inner complexes to which the artist felt preordained by fate. This trait, even obsession, brushed aside every obstacle to its expression, thus reducing art form to its simplest, and, in its very bareness, most effective elements, such as line and colour. These did not, however, serve to build up form to stand as an abstraction between the creator and the world, but were to render 'direct' proof. Munch was, undoubtedly, in this respect, a predecessor of Expressionism, just as he himself followed up the spiritual legacy of Vincent van Gogh's painting, with which he early came into contact, in fact, during his second stay in Paris, which he began in the year 1889 as a twenty-six year old Norwegian fellowship holder.

R. A. Heller has shown how Munch, even when confronted with public opposition, did not shrink from the attempt to base the emotions he expressed in painting on certain stories and symbols alluding to ancient mythological models. For, at heart, he was convinced that art should have a communicative function.[14] His work, nonetheless, has passed an important dividing line, which makes it truly 'modern'. The remaining traditional themes were drowned in a flood of emotionality, which gains its strength not from merely interpreting passing experiences but from issuing, irresistibly and unchangeably, from the very depths of the artist's psyche. The tragedy of this novel concept of art consists in the fact that all current criteria of professionality disappeared at this point. Art became the ultimate means through which the desire to live took expression. It became the lifeline, which the artist's desperate self grasped hold of as it was being swept away by the undercurrents and whirlpools of life. Such an interpretation is no exaggeration in the cases of Munch and Van Gogh. Their art arose from explicitly personal sources, and its greatness stems from their feeling that personal tragedy is the tragedy of humanity as a whole.

The beginnings of Munch's typical form of expression appear in works such as 'Shout' (1893). Munch himself suggestively described the actual experience which gave rise to this penetrating picture, executed in a number of techniques. 'I was walking along a road with two friends, and the sun was setting. The sky was suddenly blood-red. I stood still and, dead tired, leant on the railings – on the blue-black fjord. Over the town there lay blood and fiery tongues. My friends walked on, and I remained behind, trembling with fear and sensing the great infinite shout of nature.'[15]

'Shout' embodies nothing literary, everything is greatly simplified in shape, and exaggerated. To a certain extent, we can understand the fury of the visitors to the notorious exhibition of Munch's works in Berlin in 1892, who wished to send Munch to a lunatic asylum, and called his pictures fraudulent. The neurotic complex which inspired this painting was, in fact, almost pathological. Its artistic expression not only relieved Munch of his dangerous inner tension but, on a broader scale, revealed the authentic experience of crisis as a general symptom of culture. In the wild battle of red-and-yellow and poisonously green colours, in the spurting recession of the terrace and the ruthlessly-placed, diagonal railings, in the convulsion of the lonely figure in the foreground, the resounding elemental movement of the sky, and the landscape of the fjord, there is expressed, in unison and in purely visual terms, the approaching catastrophe of the world, below the surface of which the mighty forces of nature are felt. The shouting figure, identifiable with Munch, is covering up his ears. He is in a position of conflict, but the shout of nature issues forth even from him. Munch's human being, in his emotional collapse, begins to identify himself with creative powers far exceeding his puny individuality. Munch's artistic 'wilfulness' that so shocked the spectators at the exhibition is, in fact, a challenge to overweening egoism. The new individualism here stretches far beyond the sphere of social conventions and morals, being aware once again of that 'original substance' of life, with which, once before, the Romantics had come into contact.

While, however, in the work of C. D. Friedrich, for example, man remained merely a kind of visitor of nature, who is allowed a quiet insight into its dark mysteries, Munch's man is essentially involved in its inner processes, because of their vital importance to him. Two dates are always stressed at the beginning of Munch's life-story, each marked with a cross. His mother died of tuberculosis when the young Munch was 5 years old, and, nine years later, his sister Sophy, to whom the young Edvard had obviously transferred much of what he would have felt for his mother, died of the same disease. Both these events were constantly in his mind. As late as 1894, he drew his mother as a faceless figure of youthful appearance leaning on the head of the bed and talking to two weeping children. This 'Childhood Memory' undoubtedly referred to the lines his dying mother left to his elder sister, in which she admonished the children to follow the Christian faith, that all of them should meet again in the kingdom of heaven. He depicted his sister during the nineties in a series of paintings on the theme of 'Sick Girl'; while his famous 'Death Rooms' show the sad end of his family.

Munch's well-known statement that he did not paint what he saw but what he had seen, is clearly demonstrable. He constantly stressed that his art was essentially based on his own experiences, and that at its core lay memories of life at home, and his reactions to the abnormal atmosphere caused by the deep fear of the inexorable disease, and by the religious pietism to which the artist's father, in his grief, resorted.

Indeed, Munch escaped to Paris, and then to Berlin, for long-term stays to rid himself of the melancholy which had so deeply marked him in childhood. But he carried it with him wherever he went. The bohemian life, the oblivion of alcohol did nothing but deepen it. Yet this escapism, apart from the fact that it led to contacts with other artists resulting in the first stirrings of modern art, became symptomatic of the inner link between his life and his work. The story of his life seems to be an expansion of the dynamic lines and intense colours of his paintings, flowing across their frame into free space.

With the lapse of time, as Munch took an increasing part in the new cultural circles forming in France and Germany, this apparently handicapping and disruptive psychic core acquired a different value. It was sublimated into works of art and culminated in paintings that became unique imprints of the tormented search for new contacts with the material springs of life by a crippled and uprooted individual.

From 1893 onwards, Munch began to sum up his themes, which had crystallized into obsessively-fixed images, into larger series which he called 'Frieze of Life'. The core of these loose poems in colour about the relationship between life and death became the image of womanhood embodied most comprehensibly as a symbol of the three psychological states of woman, seen in her significance for man and for life in its basic time dimension (R. A. Heller). Munch depicted woman as an innocent, yearning virgin in white garments, then as a nude lover in the full development of her vital strength, and, finally, as a dark-clothed mother-widow. Preceding this ultimate treatment of the whole theme, apparently influenced by the endeavour to meet the beholder half-way and help him understand the picture, there were less comprehensible records and forms that were perhaps difficult even for Munch himself to decipher. The first of these is probably a drawing from the year 1893, which represents three closely-set female heads, giving the impression of a mythological monster, whose faces with closed eyes are immersed in sleep. While the outer two faces are light, almost transparent, and their expression more relaxed, the central one is framed in dark hair, giving a sad effect, and its expression is one of pain. If this drawing, too, is related to the problem of the confrontation of man and time, so typical of Munch, then its time dimension is of a somewhat different kind than that of the image of the cycle of a woman's life as fixed in the general view of the contemplating man-artist. The subject here is not the development of life, but the transformation of two basic psychic states – suffering, dark introversion, and luminous serenity. It is a matter of guessing why this serenity was represented symmetrically in the two outer heads. But if we accept in advance the idea that such drawings by Munch as the woman with three heads were, indeed, works most closely related to the inner images of the artist himself, that they were the most intimate records of his personal imagination, then we must once again consider the personal sources of Munch's imagination and recall the two losses he suffered in childhood. This is further upheld by the fact that, while Munch might well have come into contact with similar mythological types in visits to museums, or from other sources, in this case no direct influence by earlier patterns has so far been shown to exist.

It is interesting that, later, this drawing was cut in half, and two further scenes were drawn on its back: a nude girl with eyes cast down or closed, and surrounded by tempting demons, and a female body, in the process of disintegration, shallowly buried in the ground. Out of the body a big grasslike plant grows with birds flying around it in the sun, and in the background two indistinct figures are bathing in a fjord. In 1897, Munch turned this drawing into a lithograph called 'Death and Life', which similarly depicts a female body lying in the ground and upward-growing roots of trees and flowers. On the surface of the ground, in the zone of life, are Munch's most pleasant motifs: an apple-tree, a girl, a pleasant-looking fjord and a brilliant sun.

In connection with these images one might quote an entry in Munch's diary, dated 8th January 1892 and dealing with a problem that was clearly close to the artist's heart, affected as he was by a prolonged reaction to his father's death. This entry refers first to the question: what is the basis of the talent every being possesses and needs to be able to develop? The answer is that it is his spirit or soul. The question then continues: in what does this spirit, this force that keeps the body together and is immortal, consist? We know that nothing is lost – an example is Nature, in which the dead body in its decay provides nourishment for new growth – but the question returns, where then is this soul, this spirit of life? That nobody can tell. To deny its existence after the death of the body is as stupid as it is to define precisely what sort of thing it is. Similarly, there is no point in pitting fanatical non-belief against fanatical belief in one faith, for instance in Christianity.

Munch's spiritual profile, as seen through these notes, and its realization in art can be called mystical pantheism.[16] However, we are not dealing with an adopted philosophical attitude, but with a gradually acquired conviction, born not from the objectivity of quiet meditation, but from the anxiety of the artist's psychic ego, threatened at its very foundations. In 1901, Munch drew the 'Empty Cross', where he assembled a number of his crisis motifs, such as the head of the 'jealous' man, the scheme of man and woman from 'Vampire', and others, under the symbol of the empty cross, a typical Jungian 'mandala', but without its anthropomorphic or deistic centre. These motifs gave proof of the psychic 'inflation' of its creator, and the threat to his mental balance through something exceeding his power of comprehension. The world, as represented here, was still a convulsive chaos, in which the individual wandered with a feeling of fear, where the last straw of salvation was love. Munch was never a herald of any old, or new, religion, just as he never created a distinct artistic programme bounded by rules and a fixed system of form. His individualism was to such an extent one of principle that it forced him to find a consistent balance for his own psychic burden and to do so unaided, on his own.

The pressing question, which significantly reappeared in his diary of the year 1892, as to where the soul is and what it consists in, indicates that Munch as an artist felt impelled to find an answer to it in visual terms also. Woman seemed to him the most natural symbol for the soul. What Munch drew and painted was not a concrete, living woman, it was not even a likeness of woman as such, but a symbolic projection of what Jung later termed 'anima'. Munch's pictures of women are gradual evocations of an archetypal, psychic picture of woman, which the artist, in view of the childhood loss of mother and sister was, to some extent, deprived of, or which he possessed, but in undeveloped form, and which had to be complemented, so that his psychic personality might acquire the necessary balance. In that sense, Munch's art was of prime importance to himself and helped to found that line in modern art which came to be labelled as Expressionist. His 'self-expression' was, of course, to a great extent, symptomatic of the crisis character of the period and, moreover, encompassed such a serious chapter in the general development of the human personality that it far exceeded the limits of individual treatment by means of art and became a message to all mankind.

In the nineties, Munch's work comprised two basic, interpenetrating circles of images. The first of them is motivated by a choking feeling of fear and loss, and the isolated man is placed in it against a setting of nature, crushing down on him, e.g. 'Shout' (1893), 'Feeling of Fear' (1896), 'Empty Cross' (1901). Similarly, in another of Munch's drawings there is a disturbed and frightened child, confronted with the mystery of death, e.g. 'Dead Mother and Child', done before 1899. The second circle dealt with the theme of love and is, in other words, the response to the first. Its culmination is the theme of 'The Kiss', several times repeated in various techniques, which, especially in the drawings of nude figures embracing at a window, most dynamically conveys Munch's longing for harmony and the merger of the male and female principle, not only as the two extremes of external 'human nature', but mainly as two integral aspects of the artist's own psyche. The flame-shaped drawing of the two bodies and their merger in a kiss again affirms how central the emotion must have been that gave rise to this picture. A beautiful drawing of a nude with a softly-marked halo around the head, suggesting a Madonna, belongs to the same cycle. While the consequent picture and lithograph have a tragic ring, the drawing itself is triumphantly sensual.

Such drawing is, of course, not really typical of Munch's work in the nineties, when all the motifs, even the apparently quite naturalistic ones, bore clear psychic significance. Munch was still trying to find a way out of his initial trauma in an exclusively mental way and, bearing in mind that sphinx of his, one can, on the whole, comprehend even such drawings as 'Fever', 'Son' (from the year 1894), and special variations of the well-known theme of 'Death Rooms'. At the bedside of a young man lying with folded hands and closed eyes there appear by the side of real figures two astral shadows, which might perhaps be deciphered as symbols of Munch's deceased. On a much later 'realistic' variation on this theme, these two shadows changed into two portrait pictures.

These considerations bring back to mind the fact that Munch's image of woman was not intended to be merely a general expression of the life relationship between man and woman, but that it was set in a far more complex psychic problem of Munch himself as its creator. The constant link with the significance of woman as mother is archetypal, and the general order of Munch's achievement should be considered in connection with this most profound of his motifs. In 1908 Munch suffered a mental breakdown, and this crisis contrives to divide his work into two different parts. In the second 'half', which continued into the thirties, woman is no longer the symbolic image of the soul and its transformations. She is seen and experienced in her physical and personal reality, she ceases to be a mystery and becomes a positive fact in life. In our context, this means that Munch had compensated for the deficient female aspect in his own psyche, that he had achieved a balance that also enabled him to see the world in its natural reality. Nor are those other women a direct continuation of their predecessors from the nineties and the beginning of the new century. The original women-images either symbolically died or became, literally, transfigured. Typical of the first cycle is the theme 'Dead Lovers', which occupied Munch in 1901; it is connected with the 'Empty Cross' and, in personal associations, terminates one of the chapters in his life. Similarly, the cyclical concept of 'Three Stages of Woman' and the 'Frieze of Life' brought to an end the significance of these images, and produced images of the infinite circulation of matter in nature, expressed in the motif of the decaying body and the plant growing out of it, which for Munch was a symbol of art. The second cycle was ushered in by the drawing of the three-headed woman, significantly related to the archetype of mother through the symbols of light and shadow, which Munch then expressed even more literally in an important lithograph 'In the Land of the Crystal' (1897). Here he dealt pictorially with the question of immortality, by dividing the picture into two zones, a dark earthly one, from which a coffin with a resurrected dead is rising up into the light zone of crystallizing buildings and trees. From the same year dates a lithograph of nudes of a man and a woman drawn among two arches, longingly levitating towards the orb of the sun, although their legs are still bound. The well-known wall painting of a brilliant sun in the assembly hall of Oslo University formed the culmination of this new symbolic trend in Munch's work which began to appear in the nineties and gradually absorbed his former idea of woman.

The victorious progress of this tendency acquires more profound meaning once we realize that the basic need of Munch's development was not only to express and solve his attitude to woman–world but also to woman–soul. Munch did not draw the old theme of the Woman Clothed with the Sun, but his intuition and creative instinct, propelled by the courage to find a consistent solution, in the end reached the balance that might be described in the words of his own comment on his work: 'The mysticism of long development, joined in one'.

25.

Edvard Munch:
Dead Mother
and Child
before 1899,
pencil and charcoal,
50 × 65 cm
T 301 Munch-museet,
Oslo

[Frontispiece]
Edvard Munch:
Shout
1893, pastel,
75 × 57 cm
OKK 122B
Munch-museet, Oslo

Edvard Munch:
The Kiss
1894/95,
pencil and Indian ink,
60.4 × 38.9 cm
T 421 Munch-museet,
Oslo

Edvard Munch:
Fever (Son)
1894, charcoal,
42.5 × 48.2 cm
T 2381, Munch-museet,
Oslo

28.

Edvard Munch:
Empty Cross
1901, Indian ink and
watercolour,
43.1 × 62.7 cm
2452 Munch-museet,
Oslo

Jan Preisler

Munch's influence had a great effect on the new art that was coming into being in Central Europe at the turn of the century. In 1905, a big Munch exhibition was held in Prague in the pavilion of the progressive Mánes Association of Artists. The poster for the exhibition was designed by the Czech painter Jan Preisler, one of its organizers. He had become acquainted with Munch's work in the middle nineties through the lively Prague 'Modern Review', which introduced the cultural circles of Prague to Symbolism, particularly to literary symbolism. St. Przybyszewski, who had been a close friend of Munch's in Berlin, became the favourite author of the Czech 'Decadents'. His short novels, obscure stories of fatefully conceived sexuality, together with translations from Huysmans, had a momentous effect on the intellectual atmosphere of the 'fin de siècle' in the vibrant city of the Austro-Hungarian Empire, striving as it was for national independence in opposition to official policy.

Preisler had a great deal in common with Munch. He had an outstanding command of colour, and even before he became acquainted with the work of the modern French painters, among whom he was later particularly attracted by Gauguin, he used pure colour to express the intensively poetical meaning of his paintings. Preisler, too, bore deep within him the burden of life's sadness, and hence his relationship to Munch was clearly that much the deeper. Imitation was quite out of the question. Instead, their affinity was based on a similarity of experience which, in Preisler's case, naturally lacked Munch's cruel, northern and existentially extrovert features and was typically Slavonic, softer and more lyrical.

Preisler's triptych 'Easter', drawn in charcoal, dates from 1896. In its central section he drew a shepherd-boy contemplating with feverishly open eyes the invisible mystery of spiritual transfiguration. The bare landscape of early spring and birch groves forms an effective setting for the visionary scene, quite in tune with the images of contemporary nature poetry. It is interesting, though, that this 'stylish' landscape, typical of Preisler's paintings, which all show an infallible feeling for the unity of figure and landscape, was not an 'ideal' one. The painter's meadows, streams and birch groves, the landscape vistas and mixed forests, even the limestone ravines with lakes, the setting for allegorical figures, are all based on the landscape of his childhood. This link is most typical of Preisler and can be found in all his works. It shows, moreover, how much Preisler's case differed from that of Munch. What the two painters had in common was an intense awareness of a void in their lives, a feeling of loss and a need to fill up the empty place in the inhospitable wasteland of the real world, into which they were cast. That was the source of their artistic innovations and of their positive participation in the new cultural groupings preparing for radical change. Yet even in this context Preisler was expressly a painter of 'Paradise Lost'.

In Preisler's work from the period around 1900 we constantly find a type of adolescent youth standing immobile, or sitting in a landscape with a distant horizon. The youth's full, symmetrical face reflects an emotional state of mind difficult to describe in words. Preisler's series of such faces forms a definite range of expressions. With a slight contraction of the corners of the mouth, or an almost imperceptible stress on the eyes, they become more melancholic, or more lively. They are examples of that special mixture of meanings typical of the period, which, with a certain playful lability, shifts emotions between passivity and resignation, and energy and vitality, between autumn and spring. A constant feature of Preisler's youths is their expectation and, notably, their listening to the silence. It might be said that Preisler's pictures are musical, or rather audio-visual, and that their synesthesia perhaps points to the later problem of modern art, which came to be filled in by Kandinski's idea of 'the resounding cosmos'.

In the silence of Preisler's drawings and pictures gentle voices can – as it were – be heard. Man, in his most sensitive state of adolescence, is here set in nature, a stylized vision of the native landscape. And nature speaks to him, nature conceived not as an Impressionist setting, and certainly not as something inimical and mysterious, but as the maternal basis of man's entire growth. The pantheistic basis of the entire relationship is much the same here as with Munch, but, contrasted with the cataclysms of the northern soul, in Preisler's work the link with the origin of life is sought in a quiet and poetically pure, lyrical relationship. Nor was Preisler's route to the new unity, which certain values tempt one to call a 'more oriental' route, certainly in its initial stages, without sorrows. A more passive abatement of introspection might have led to ossification of the image, but Preisler faced this danger of mental catatonia with a quite unusual emotional ardour. Among contemporaries, Preisler at times comes close to the slightly older Belgian painter Fernando Khnoppf, who also drew motionless, concentrating faces. But in Khnoppf's work the motif led to the theme of 'The Head of Medusa' (c. 1895) and its significance was shifted to a sphere of bewitchment and negative influence.

The hiatus in Preisler's approach lay in the oppressively-felt contradiction between reality and the ideal. It was a psychic sorrow arising from non-fulfilment. Preisler reached the bottom of this sadness most intensively in the illustrations accompanying the 'Song of the Sorrow of the Good Youth Roman Vasilich' written by the Czech Symbolist poet Julius Zeyer. The Russian scenery formed an easily understandable frame for passionate readers of Dostoevsky and Chekhov, and Preisler sensitively evoked the content of the ballad that dealt ruefully with the inner disintegration of the young hero. It is a very sensitive account of spiritual conflict, in which the poet and the illustrator come to a congenial understanding in dealing with the problem of the hero's fated propensity towards self-negation.

Preisler's fixedly-gazing youths can be understood as symbols of the apparently balanced psychic state, which, in reality, is the moment of greatest concentration before a major decision. It is a moment when the scales move almost imperceptibly, and the adolescent poses to himself, and through himself, a basic question. Preisler also depicted here a series of finely differentiated figures and faces, in which, as in a true mirror, an inner process of decision-making is taking place, hidden to superficial view by the repetitive stereotype of the picture. This process is further complicated as the picture simultaneously acquired certain qualities of style which, in their turn, are far from any patterns of forms. As the content of Preisler's drawings and paintings becomes more compact, these spontaneous marks of style become proportionately more refined, e.g. the curved lines of briar rose or blackberry canes, contrasted with the frontal symmetry of the slightly stylized faces, or the constantly more intense impact of the colour composition, which rapidly departed from the local colour scheme.

The intuitive wealth of Preisler's expression was simultaneously made possible and redeemed by his entire pictorial world being shifted into the realm of poetical fiction, into the fairy-tale. The romantic impulse can be seen in Preisler's work from the nineties when his typical theme, the lonely figure of a man confronted with voices from life and nature, embodied in the half-real girls–fairies first appeared in the 'Cycle of the Adventurous Knight'. Some pictures belonging to this cycle are somewhat puzzling, due to the contrast of the imaginary subject-matter and sharp luminarism, imported from Paris. Soon afterwards, a major integration took place in Preisler's work, which led to the origin of the masterly 'Picture from a Larger Cycle' (1902). It was in this painting that Preisler showed himself as a modern colourist. And, at the same time, there began the significant silent dialogue between the typical youth, given in profile, and the poetical figure of the girl looking up at him. Her opalescent garment and the bird alighted on it show that it is a personification of the soul of the native country, which is turning the spirit of adventure of youth towards itself. Beginning with this picture, Preisler began to devote himself to the theme of 'Lovers' and his idea was further developed in the important 'Black Lake' (1904), until it reached its monumental culmination. In 'Black Lake', which the painter himself called 'Melancholy', the theme of a rider entered the repertory of Preisler's images, and this dynamic element seems to suggest that the magic of loneliness was to be broken and that the future programme was to be the attainment of a complete balance of the basic forces in life, which then, e.g. in 'Adam and Eve' (1908), came to be expressed in a grandiose decorative composition, reminiscent of Gauguin.

In connection with this general transformation colour came to assume a major significance in Preisler's work. In its new orchestrations it was to enable the painter to express his dream of life. Typical of this change is the shift of the colour-scheme from the silvery, lunar colours of the early melancholic works, where black played an important role, to the yellow-green, solar colours of the later works, whose subject-matter turned to the theme of optimism in life. In drawing, too, Preisler's general development can be clearly detected when he turned from the trend towards linear and flat stylization as two distinct values to three-dimensional depiction, as in his later drawings of nudes. Once again, the question of his relationship to the European tradition is a topical one.

29.

Jan Preisler:
Easter, central
part of triptych
1896, charcoal,
55 × 43 cm
G 6412 Gallery
of Fine Arts, Olomouc

Jan Preisler:
Knight-Errant
*before 1902, charcoal
and white chalk,
36.3 × 40.6 cm
K 5387 National
Gallery, Prague*

Jan Preisler:
Illustration to Julius
Zeyer's poem 'Song
of the Sorrow
of the Good Youth
Roman Vasilich'
1899, black chalk,
23 × 37.5 cm
K 34632 National
Gallery, Prague

Jan Preisler:
Illustration to Jan
Neruda's poem
1902, charcoal
and white chalk,
58.5 × 46 cm
K 36314 National
Gallery, Prague

33·

Jan Preisler:
Sketch for
a ceiling picture
*1910, pastel,
46 × 46 cm
K 30693 National
Gallery, Prague*

Jan Preisler:
Two Reclining Nudes
*1910, charcoal
and white chalk,
39.5 × 54.4 cm
K 13363 National
Gallery, Prague*

František Bílek

Symbolism found fertile ground in Czech cultural circles, and out of it grew the interesting work of František Bílek, a sculptor and graphic artist. At the age of eighteen, in 1890, Bílek went to Paris, and though he stayed there only until October 1892, he became acquainted, mainly through his fellow countryman Mucha, with the French movement at the very moment of its heroic début. For Bílek, highly moralist by nature, those aspects of Symbolism which re-instated the problem of the artist's attitude to religion became most attractive. Throughout his long and highly creative life he concentrated on this issue.

The young Bílek experienced his 'entry into life' as a major personal crisis. The first works he modelled in Paris, entitled 'Golgotha – Mount of Skulls' and 'Ploughing is Punishment for our Guilt' were marked by a naturalism which gave Bílek's christological themes such unaccustomed sharpness that the Prague Commission withdrew his scholarship. This only deepened Bílek's general depression, in which, however, there flickered an inextinguishable flame of resistance, kept alive by an almost chiliastic conviction of the instability of the external world, which inclined him towards visionary mysticism. Bílek never hesitated to commit heresy as soon as some of the ecclesiastical and cultural currents, with which he successively came into contact, endeavoured to limit the freedom of his own conviction. Bílek thus became a typical representative of those artists who were extremely attracted by the redeeming idea of service to supra-personal ideals, and yet who, at the same time, firmly insisted that they themselves were the authentic prophets of such redemption.

In view of Bílek's general attitude, it is understandable that Christ became the central figure of his iconography in the nineties. It was not, of course, the beautiful Christ of the Romantic Classicism of the 19th century. On the contrary, Bílek's Christ came from that romantic and tragic family of heroes who were not representatives but seekers, and, therefore, also martyrs and sufferers. A quotation from Oscar Wilde shows that this theme was attractive at the time. It was written after Wilde's humiliation by the English court:

'If ever I write again, in the sense of producing artistic work, there are just two subjects on which and through which I desire to express myself: one is "Christ as the precursor of the romantic movement in life", the other is "The artistic life considered in its relation to conduct". The first is, of course, intensely fascinating, for I see in Christ not merely the essentials of the supreme romantic type, but all the accidents, the wilfulness even, of the romantic temperament also. He was the first person who ever said to people that they should live "flower-like lives". ... And feeling, with the artistic nature of one to whom suffering and sorrow were modes through which he could realise his conception of the beautiful, that an idea is of no value till it comes incarnate and is made an image, he made of himself the image of the Man of Sorrows, and as such has fascinated and dominated art as no Greek god ever succeeded in doing.'[17]

Bílek comprehended Christ primarily in that romantic tradition, conceiving him also as the 'Son of Man', as the symbol of the human moral problem. Wilde's statement shows how this newly-roused interest presented the need to see Christ, not only as a personal example, but as a more generally valid artistic and living form. Bílek, too, in the nineties inevitably moved from naturalistic analysis towards a more comprehensive synthesis in his view of the world. His 'Crucified' (1896—99) became a monument to this change in his art. The genesis of this large-sized wood-carving, with preparatory drawings, can be traced in Bílek's correspondence with the poet Julius Zeyer, who was a spiritually close friend to him at that time.[18] It reveals that, at the beginning, the statue was conceived as a drastic and illusionist picture of Jesus's physical suffering and his death, which in Bílek's over-sensitive messianic psychism was to make a direct impact upon the beholder, persecute him mentally and convince him of his complicity in the human tragedy. Zeyer, however, criticized this concept in the sense that the aim of the statue was not to be a depiction of death, but triumph over death, showing the spiritual path by means of light radiating from the crucified as a mark of his divinity. This departure from naturalism meant that the work of art was conceived as a symbolist project, with stress being mainly laid on the deliberate symbol of light as the main bearer of this new significance.

Bílek's symbolism of light has a dual aspect. One relates to the influence of the literary tradition drawn in the first place from the basic religious source, the Bible. When Bílek explained the real programme of his relief 'The Significance of the Word Madonna' he used current religious metaphors: 'In fact, the relationship of the Virgin Mary to Christ. I lead the spectator to a page in the New Testament. I open the Holy Writ up for him, the Gospel according to St. John I. And I let him read: how He, the same, the unchangeable, the Divine, in the very beginning, before everything was made, was complete; how He will be born, how He is to live and die; in the very beginning was He, "the Light", the sun of our souls, which in our dark time through our Moon – the Virgin Mary – is to embrace the world. The impressions this reading rouses are drawn in this book... The world then turned into a coarse sleeper, who does not welcome the Light of God coming through the Virgin Mary, turns away testily, and with the clouds, his own darkness, covers that radiance to sleep the more easily.'[19] At the same time this originally literary significance is treated truly artistically and becomes one of the main stimuli for the development of the artist's own imagination.

In the year 1899 Bílek drew a large-sized cartoon, entitled 'Mother!'. The very subject of this fantastic drawing speaks for itself. In the dark night, with a large, pale moon rising over the horizon, a part of a mighty tree-trunk stretching across the entire height of the drawing breaks off; it seems to be its soul, lit up and shining. It assumes the likeness of a human face, with the closed eyes of a sleep-walker and a serene expression of deliverance, which seems to be rising towards a star shimmering faintly above it high in the sky. The symbolism of light in the drawing interprets the effective mystery of the trans-substantiation, of a quiet, spiritual and, at the same time, natural event, whose poetical depth transcends allusions to current religious metaphors. It becomes an artistic parallel to the words of another of Bílek's friends, the poet Otakar Březina, whose acquaintance he made in 1901: 'The invisible world infiltrates into the visible world. Through the freedom of the dream, art intervenes in the explanation

·of things…The light it pours over the objects is purer and more enigmatic than the light of our sun: it is the other, spiritual, side of this light…' Březina wrote these sentences in his essays which belong to the most original and valuable assertions of the Czech movement. They were, however, not published until the year 1905.[20]

The genesis of Bílek's symbolism of light might have been patterned on Odilon Redon, with whose work he came into contact through a mutual friend, the artist Zdenka Braunerová. What was most important was that Bílek elaborated all these different sources until they turned into an integral attitude which, at the beginning of the new century, developed into a unique form of mythology.

The manner in which Bílek expressed his view of the world is by linking symbolically-comprehended light with matter. Such a link, conceived as the emanation of spiritual light into the darkness of dead matter, i.e. in a neo-Platonic manner, is clearest to Bílek in the central sphere of living nature, i.e. in the shaping of man. Bílek's statues from the beginning of the century, and, in particular, his depiction of John Huss, the national martyr burnt at the stake by the Council of Constance, defy Classicism. The figure of Huss, growing out of a tree-trunk, with eyes mystically closed and hair flowing, changes into a flame kindled within him, in Bílek's imagination, by immense cosmic energy, towards which he is drawn upwards in a dynamic, arched curve. The merger of figure and tree is another typical point in Bílek's mythology, faithfully continuing the significance that tradition ascribed to this symbol of life. Everywhere, light is conceived as an eminently power-producing factor, which lights up a spiritual fire in people and stimulates the whole of nature to growth. Bílek entitled the· Huss statue 'The Tree which, struck by Lightning, Burnt throughout the Ages'.

Bílek's linking of the figure and the tree shows that his sculptor's *taille directe* had strikingly ideoplastic assumptions. At the same time, it is connected with the contemporary *Art Nouveau* style, which, in a similar manner, broadened the effect of plant forms. In Bílek's work the tree, of course, changes into a man, so that the traditional hierarchy, based on advancing growth towards spirituality, was maintained, while the contemporary, decorative regression to floral and ornamental forms was expressly rejected. These relations of meaning were at times shifted, as can be shown, for example, in Bílek's 'Places of Harmony and Reconciliation' (1900), where a pair of pilgrims who have landed on a riverbank in a little, heart-shaped boat, find themselves faced with an avenue of tall trees, whose tops change into figures with raised arms, thus forming a vaulted nave, through which a hand of light reveals itself to the pilgrims. This drawing can be compared with a model of the nave for the church of La Sagrada Familia in Barcelona by Antonio Gaudí (1925), which was never built, where the support pillars of the nave are treated as stylized, spreading trees. What, in Bílek's work, is a Symbolist fantasy became a symbolic artistic structure in the work of Gaudí, but the ideoplastic basis of these two works is identical.

In a number of other statues and drawings by Bílek one can easily distinguish typical *Art Nouveau* curves, which Bílek himself explained as lines signifying 'spiritual embraces'. For example, the drawings for Bílek's

'The Lord's Prayer' (1901) are undoubtedly marked by the ornamental trends of his time. But it must be claimed that these values were creatively authentic. Bílek, in reality, was not so much involved in contemporary efforts to achieve a homogeneous artistic style, as in the spiritual and formal preparation and realization of an already established style. Bílek knew the work of William Blake, and was undoubtedly influenced a good deal by it, both as to ideas and form. Blake's influence is suggested by Bílek's basic inclination towards the light element of fire, dynamically contrasting with the softening of Blake's curve in *Art Nouveau*. Bílek's expression was shaped, of course, by the apocalyptic feeling of the end of the century, and, for that reason, his mythological world was not at all the complex allegory of Olympus. Bílek constantly confronted man with his insecure position among contradictory forces and made it his task to encourage man's longing for reconciliation with these forces by his general elevation. He never hesitated to apply all the sources of religious knowledge and history for this purpose. The core of his art is the ennoblement of man's emotional substance through his attainment of a higher state. In this way his work represents a demand for a work of art to be imbued with elemental spiritual strength.

36.

František Bílek:
Places of Harmony
and Reconciliation
1900, charcoal,
191 × 102.5 cm
G 1080 Gallery of the
City of Prague,
Prague

František Bílek:
How Time Gives
Us Wrinkles
1902, charcoal,
132.5 × 155.2 cm
G 1083 Gallery of the
City of Prague,
Prague

František Bílek:
Women Invoking
*1901, pencil
and blue pencil,
61 × 44.3 cm
K 33530 National
Gallery, Prague*

František Bílek:
Reading Begins with
the Letters
of the Figure
Introductory page of
a drawn tractate
on the human figure
Indian ink and white,
44.4 × 34 cm
K 41197 National
Gallery, Prague

POCETA CETRA
PISMENA TELA CLOVEKA:

Alfred Kubin

The trend towards the fantastic, which was so typical of art at the turn of the 19th and 20th centuries, found perhaps its most consistent representative in the Austrian Alfred Kubin. Kubin worked until the middle of this century, but the core of his art, or rather the psychic melting-pot from which his fantastic visions emerged, belongs unmistakably to the period forming the dividing line between two worlds. Furthermore, Kubin's work shows a pronounced association with a particular place because, in its entirety, his work is a quite extraordinary reflection of the inner collapse of the century-old monarchy on the banks of the Danube.

Kubin had, without doubt, the most unstable temperament of all the artists that we are dealing with. His dream psychosis[21] emerged in childhood and affected him deeply during puberty, culminating in an hysterical attempt at suicide on his mother's grave. Even before this, his entirely unadaptable personality had developed a sharp antagonism towards other persons, their company and their attitudes, one form of which was hatred for his father, and was compensated by various sadistic eccentricities. He was, in fact, forced to leave the Salzburg secondary school before completion of his course, since he proved quite incapable of concentration on his work. This condition became further aggravated when he had his first collapse in a psychotic storm a few days after voluntarily enlisting in the army. Kubin had a second attack in Munich where he attended the Academy of Fine Arts.

The career of artist was clearly the only possible one in view of his entire mental and physical condition. During this second acute crisis he was strongly affected by a cycle of prints by Max Klinger, 'The Lost Glove', through which his distraught fantasy can be said to have been given a degree of artistic support. Klinger's introspective work, strangely linking Naturalism and the dream atmosphere of the hallucinatory story, clearly provided Kubin with the impulse to express his own states and experiences more vividly. Klinger's unusual manner of unfolding images, which followed Goya's 'Caprichos', must have been attractive to young Kubin in his search for the means of crystallizing his own chaotic world. This initiation into the mystery of one of the most outstanding undercurrents in the development of European art was quite authentically intuitive in Kubin's case. In his autobiography he described in detail what happened to him immediately after seeing Klinger's prints:

'With my heart still full I roamed about the town and in the evening went to a music hall, for I was looking for an indifferent, yet noisy environment in order to even out the inner pressure that kept intensifying. There, something mentally very strange and decisive for me occurred, which I cannot fully grasp to this day although I have given a great deal of thought to it. As the small orchestra began to play, my entire environment became suddenly clear and more distinct, as in a different light. Suddenly I saw in the faces of those sitting about me odd, human-animal features; all sounds were peculiarly strange, disjoined from their causes; I seemed to hear what sounded to me like a scoffing, moaning, booming general tongue that I could not understand, but which seemed to possess a clear, ghostly, inner meaning. I became sad, although a strange feeling of bliss flooded through me; and, again, I thought of Klinger's prints, while considering what work I should now be doing. And then, suddenly, a whole flood of visions of black-and-white pictures poured over me – it is impossible to describe what thousandfold wealth appeared in my imagination. I quickly left the theatre, for the music and the many lights now disturbed me, and wandered aimlessly through the dark streets, all the time overpoweringly in the grasp of, literally held captive by, a dark power which conjured up in my mind's eye strange animals, houses, landscapes, grotesque and terrible situations. I felt indescribably well and ennobled in my enchanted world, and when I became tired of running about, I entered a small tea-room. Here, too, everything was quite out of the ordinary. On entering, it seemed as if the waitresses were wax-dolls moving by god knows what mechanism, and as if I had surprised the few guests – who appeared to me unreal, like shadows – at some satanic business. The entire background, with the orchestrina and the buffet, seemed suspicious. It appeared to me like a dummy which was meant to hide the secret proper, presumably a dimly-lit, bloody, stable-like cave. What I was able to catch of these images, which changed surprisingly easily while I myself remained entirely passive, I drew with a few rapid strokes in my sketch-book. The inner agitation continued on my way home, the Augustenstrasse seemed to shrink on its own accord, and a mountain range seemed to grow in an immense circle around our town. At home I fell into bed as though dead, and slept soundly and without dreams right to the evening of the next day. For some time afterwards I lived in seclusion.'[22]

The starting point of Kubin's art was, in other words, a profound experience of alienation, depersonalization and fantastic clairvoyance. These processes were undeniably products of his psychosis, but what is more important is that, in the repeated attacks, his artistic projection played an increasingly greater role, and, in a certain way, sublimated the products of his disturbed mind. In the autumn of 1908, Kubin wrote a remarkable novel 'Die andere Seite' during such a crisis and illustrated it himself. In this novel, while describing a visit to a mysterious, inaccessible and occult 'Realm of Dreams', somewhere in Asia, Kubin gives a summary of his experience of the reverse side of the world of phenomena and of its unstable foundations, which constantly threaten to shatter and sweep away all that is ordinary and rational in life. Under their thin surface Kubin discovered the uncontrolled ferment of instinctive and non-rational forces penetrating through the pores of the outer world of appearance, and showing themselves in their multi-dimensional, non-human logic as fiendish and fatal. With Kubin, as in the case of his great contemporary, James Ensor, the surface of his life is constantly cracking under the pressure of demoniacal forces which, at first isolated in grotesque hallucinations, gradually enter more and more into his picture of reality, and so splinter it from within.

In the case of Kubin, this development is connected with a change in technique. The first, large group of his early works is an illusively sombre record of visions arising from his experiences of profound dread. They are 'photographic' works, not only in the sense that they show the influence of Kubin's early training in photography with his uncle at Klagenfurt, but also in the way they anticipate Dali's pictures of 'concrete irrationality'. In the second group, which includes all Kubin's mature works, this gloomy and fantastic 'camera obscura' disappears, and the weight of his own graphic element increases. This change is of profound significance, because the abandonment of painterly elements and the attainment of pure, black-and-white, graphic features of drawing was felt by Kubin himself to be a new development, an artistic metaphor of constant struggle in the world. In 'Die andere Seite' he wrote: 'The repellent and attractive forces, the poles of the Earth and their currents, the change of the seasons, day and night, black and white – that is struggle'. In the spirit of these sentences, at the time when Expressionist trends appeared in art in the first decade of the 20th century, Kubin became, in 1909, a member of the Munich Neue Künstlervereinigung. His art changed. From fantastic images which intensified the effects of traditional grotesques, he advanced in his graphic work to a maximum effectiveness, in which the fantastic emerged only from the confusion of lines put on the white surface of the paper with a penetrating sense for the magic core of artistic revelation.

Kubin's fantasies were largely concerned with expressing the relationship of man to animals. A frequent theme was the threat to a tiny human figure from a monstrous animal, grotesque and huge as in a dream. It described the imminent moment of struggle, and the fear of being attacked. Kubin's inclination towards bestiality culminated in his images of a type of inverted centaur, with an animal head and human body ('The Cat Man'), and in his liking for depicting wild human types. The other aspect of Kubin's work was his sarcastic humour. At times the artist came to the very brink of caricature, and later, under the influence of the Vienna pictures of Pieter Brueghel, he broadened the image in epic manner, in the cycle 'Sansara'. Even though his later work seemed to come closer to the real scenery of the world, it always remained imbued with an exciting force, the sources of which Kubin sought in his fertile childhood experiences. It is saturated with a corrosive protest which spared no one, not even the man who made it.

40.

Alfred Kubin:
Spottbild
pastel and Indian ink,
31 × 39.6 cm
K 17350 National
Gallery, Prague

41.

Alfred Kubin:
Scorpion
Indian ink,
31.5 × 19.7 cm
K 17349 National
Gallery, Prague

Alfred Kubin:
Memory of a Trip
to Dalmatia
after 1908,
Indian ink,
36 × 26.5 cm
K 31888 National
Gallery, Prague

František Kupka

Kupka is known as one of the founders of abstract painting. His 'Amorpha – Two Coloured Fugue', exhibited at the Autumn Salon in Paris in 1912, showed its maker in a new light. Before this, Kupka had been regarded simply as one of the more skilful illustrators working for the press and for bibliophiles in ingeniously refined but otherwise traditional art forms. It was not, however, a matter of a sudden change, brought about by outside influence. His abstract painting differed considerably from the work of the generation of younger artists who in those years flooded the Paris scene with the latest '-isms'. When a contemporary critic accused Kupka of Futurism, he was judging him only by an analogy of external form. At that time, Kupka had nothing at all in common with the civilistic–machinistic euphoria of the Italians. The one thing they shared, which can only now be properly appreciated, and only in a wider context, was interest in movement and its interpretation in the picture.

Guillaume Apollinaire showed a greater understanding of Kupka's painting when he labelled it, and the non-objective pictures of R. Delaunay, with the new term 'Orphism'. The musicality of 'pure' colours and shapes seemed to be a good description of Kupka, who possessed a strong feeling of rhythm. But, in spite of this understanding and appreciation, Kupka did not, in fact, fit into the new programmes of the young Paris avant-garde. He was too much of a 'philosopher', while they were primarily interested in tangible facts of art and life. A true rapprochement did not occur until later, when in the early thirties, Kupka was elected to the presidium of the Abstraction-Création group. It was only in the thirties that his basic conception of an abstract picture as a non-orthodox depiction of the cosmos became gradually better appreciated and understood as a conception that essentially grew out of contemporary views of the world, an idea which, not only in time but in conception, preceded the endeavours of the avant-garde. Kupka's abstract painting, indeed, emerged quite organically out of the problems of art at the turn of the century, out of the reservoir of emotions and thoughts amassed by Symbolism and *Art Nouveau*.

Kupka came to Paris in 1895, after having studied at the Academies of Prague and Vienna. In both these places, a deliberate new art movement had not yet started. He acquired at the academies only academic routines, traditions kept alive in Prague by memories of the former Nazarenism, and in Vienna grown ostentatious and refined in salon fashion à la Makart. More important for his further development were the ideas he investigated, towards which he was guided by his ever-dissatisfied, ever-meditating disposition. In Prague he had grown interested in Spiritualism, and he never abandoned this interest in occult knowledge, even though, later, he subjected it to rational criteria and the imperative of the period to make it 'scientific'. This interest in the Other World was linked with his sharp criticism of existing social conditions. Kupka was a convinced anarchist and expressed his firm protest against international capital, state ideologies, religious superstitions and degradation of all kinds emphatically in several graphic cycles, which he circulated publicly. In addition, he read Nietzsche, and also Schopenhauer, whose critical pessimism was deeply attractive to those who, like Kupka, were painfully aware of the sharp contradiction between the heights of ideal, spiritual claims, and the distressing quagmire of everyday life. Kupka earned a living as an illustrator and, once he became well-known, was paid high fees, but his ambition and dissatisfaction clamoured for higher aims.

The circumstances under which Kupka joined the progressive current of art show that it was not a matter of technical problems that guided this skilful painter towards new solutions. Kupka always gave a great deal of thought to his projects, each of his pictures was prepared in detail and, as can be seen, especially in the later ones, he always clung to a certain basic theme, which he then experimented with in different variations and transformations. This approach shows Kupka as, basically, an ideoplastic type of artist, who, while pursuing the old ideal of the 'scholarly' artist, at the same time significantly altered the originally humanist ideal. In the introduction to his treatise, 'Creation in the Fine Arts', Kupka divided painting and sculpture into two large groups: the first comprised works of realistic, or secular, art, where only the impression of forms of a natural work is depicted and the artist turns his attention exclusively to the values of perceptions and impressions received from the external world; the second group contains those works of idealist, or spiritual, art, which embody a certain speculative idea appearing in a combination of plastic or coloured elements. This second type of art wishes to imbue matter with a supra-sensual idea of the unknown as it has always appeared, in greater or lesser intensity, in poetic or religious dreams.

Although Kupka himself was, undoubtedly, in favour of the second, idealistic, type of art, the very concept, 'idea', presented him with a highly complicated problem. He definitely did not mean a rationalist justification, even less an ideological scheme. On the contrary, the basically individualist and anarchist disposition of Kupka's personality laid great stress on the intuitive and independent aspects of the artist's subjective vision. Another important factor was Kupka's increasing conviction of the psycho-physical interconnections of artistic creation. He took a dilettante interest in physiology and did not hesitate to apply a positivist idea about the significance of environment to show the multiple levels of the act of creation, resulting in a work of art, and to demonstrate from what differing sources the impulses of an artistically-disposed person spring. Kupka includes under the term intelligence the talents of the senses. By creation he understands in the final analysis the co-ordination of the entire human organism, oriented by a certain predisposition to pictorial impressionability, to lyricism. Only by applying all human faculties does a work of art come into being, which 'is to be a comprehensive unity, an organism with its own special qualities of existence, which lives its own life and has a status of its own'.

These views were fully realized in Kupka's abstract painting and, at the same time, they are a bridge to his earlier, figural, Symbolist works. At the beginning, these had an expressly illustrative character. The water-colour triptych, 'The Soul of the Lotus', which takes the spectator into an exotic and spiritual region that was very attractive at the time, might be considered a pictorial complement to what Kupka later wrote in the introduction to his treatise. Here, too, the whole is divided into opposing areas, in one of which secular sensuality predominates, while the opposite one is flooded with a bright spirituality of light. The trend towards unification is expressed here through the dimension of human longing, told as a story or, as Kupka himself would say, 'allegorically'. Nonetheless, the central neutral area of the triptych, giving a rhythm to the psychically 'void' interval between two worlds, is a typical feature of *Art Nouveau*. It expresses the prevailing practice of breaking up the Classical, centrally-arranged composition; and, through its meaningful 'void', which in reality is the main part of the picture, impressing a general sense of weariness of life, it leads the spectator's eye into the unknown distance. Similarly, the motif of the lotus bud as a symbol must be considered. A coloured etching, entitled 'The Beginning of Life' and dating from the year 1903, shows a vision of two intersecting circles of light above a budding lotus. In one circle, there is a human embryo connected by the umbilical cord with a brilliant maternal object placed in the other circle. This vision, remotely reminiscent of Redon, was rightly linked to the picture 'The First Step' (1909), with which Kupka's abstract painting proper began, as with some token of cosmological speculation.[23]

The metaphysical line of Kupka's development presents the motif of the second, spiritual birth, and, in its longing for infinity and for movement within it, quite logically leads to the earth-creating nature of Kupka's vision (Kupka later wrote that each artist has the urge to create the universe anew). It is, however, complemented and complicated, by another mental plane growing out of the more sarcastic and mysterious sides of Kupka's personality.

Around the year 1900 Kupka was not only intent on exposing social evil and putting what he felt to be the outrages of the ruling classes and their ideologies into the pillory; he was also occupied with drawing demons. He drew sorcerers and witches, hags, people crushed in a mortar, a young female demon sleeping, surrounded by the shadows of human skeletons. On a hotel bill he sketched a corpse. He turned also to evoke the life of prehistoric people, expressing with a slightly bitter, slightly sadistic grin the character of the founders of the human race. The place of Adam and Eve is taken by semi-apes, their ugly figures and grimaces drawn with great academic ingenuity and illusionist precision. Their features are vividly redolent of animal lust, and an ineradicable taste for malevolence, crime and violence. Nor did Kupka have any great illusions about the origin of art. 'We can clearly imagine our remote ancestor wiping his hand, stained with the blood of the enemy he had just killed, on the wall of the cave. Then we see how, with his forefinger dipped in the same blood, he does a drawing to express his victory, and the purple patches bear the marks of his assuaged fury. Can we not further see that he showed similar intentions in the decoration of weapons, tools and tattooing, and in making effective ornaments?'

Animal instinct, and the most subtle and unearthly spirituality. These are the two contradictions between which Kupka's early work oscillates. This merciless conflict frames the space within which Kupka's art proper began to take shape.

In 1902 Kupka finished a painting for which he foresaw great artistic promise. (The picture, in fact, gained a gold medal at the World Exhibition in St. Louis in 1902.) It bears the paradoxical title 'Joys – A Ballad'.

Two nude women appear on the seashore at ebb-tide, in the light of the setting sun. One, undoing her fair hair, is sitting on a big, heavy, dappled horse, the other, dark-haired and more rigorous, bends forward as she stands on a neighing pony. The Naturalist elements of this Symbolist picture arise entirely out of Kupka's personal experiences: the landscape comes from the the scenery of Trégastel, where Kupka liked to spend his holidays, the two women are figures from Kupka's life – the dark-haired one was his French consort at that time, the blond one a Danish woman to whom Kupka had been attached in the past over a period of several years. The purely personal level in the meaning of the picture was only the starting point for its more general significance. Kupka revealed the key to it in a letter to a friend, the poet Svatopluk Machar, who lived in Vienna: 'I would like to express, in ingeniously simple manner, the feelings I used to have when I was sitting comfortably on the shore; and, as I have a great number of studies for such things, I started the work. There are two rather ugly women on horseback who come galloping along the seashore and are captivated by the warm reflection of the setting sun. The entire seashore and the clouds are attuned to some unknown joy, and in the clouds, moreover, it is as if thousands of gnomes were dancing and jumping around joyfully – we all long for some joy – a pure non-material feeling of bliss. I would like everybody who sees this thing, when it becomes a painting, to have similar feelings. After all, I want to do a work which is to mark the progress of art generally.'[24]

The scene on the picture is shifted to a mythological level by the elemental character of the landscape, in which the bare earth and the sea are confronted with an atmosphere imbued with the special, flat effect of weakening sunlight, as well as by the unusual type of horses. The naturalism of personal memories, and the mercilessly drawn nudes, sinks into this unreality, as the hooves of the horses sink in the sand on the beach bared by the ebbing tide. On the beach, strips of damp sand, lines of seaweed and the crests of the waves form typical *Art Nouveau* curves receding into the distance. These show that what was elsewhere formalized into pure ornament, was originally of symbolical meaning, linking the concept of time, as infinitely occurring continuity, with certain other attributes. The spiral-shaped, changeable dividing line between the two elements suggests the motif of the labyrinth, and thus – through the ancient association with the shape of the snake's body – a motif of elemental, vital strength, which concerns not only man, but the entire cosmos. Its might is here expressed by the sun, and particularly by sunlight as the bearer of energy, which is so much stressed in the whole picture. The colourfulness of the picture is, indeed, entirely subordinated to this content and is stressed to the maximum by the choice of an unusual technique – encaustic wax.

When we consider this picture we can understand the 'personal hypothesis' which Kupka discussed in his treatise, the proposition that perceiving an object was simply an encounter with vital energy, and, further, that visual percepts in their variety and scope perhaps contributed most to the broadening of consciousness, and to intelligence. In 'Joys – A Ballad', an idea is expressed which was to be realized later in abstract paintings, namely, that the world is an emanation of vital cosmic energy, and the picture an artistic symbol of this eternal action.

In this painting, Kupka's personal experiences in life still stand in the foreground, symbolized by the women on horseback. But also expressed is the moment when this experience literally enters the eternal zone of time, where the transformation of the main elements occurs. The 'movement' of these elements is directed by a cosmic power, which itself is of changeable and dynamic character, that is, motivating and inexhaustible. This is the source of the symbol of the horses, which Jung, for example, considered an eminently cultural symbol, a 'libido that entered the world' and is to be 'sacrificed'. Kupka himself was obviously not aware of all these facts, but, led by intuition, he grasped the essential. Furthermore, the metaphysical joy that he wrote about in the commentary to the picture shows clearly that a wide range of feelings for life had been released within him, and that, intuitively, he had achieved some kind of new totality and sense of his existence.

The drawings for 'Joys – A Ballad' which have survived on the whole confirm this analysis. Particularly interesting are the studies of the dark-haired Gabrielle, in the sense that in this figure are concentrated the visual images linked with Kupka's actual experience. There are drawings of her face, masterly examples of the meaningful polyvalence of the physiognomical Symbolism of the time, and also studies showing her nude in an energetic squatting posture. Here Kupka, in 1901 or 1902, achieved something that was developmentally important. Drawings using traditional foreshortening of the bodily contours were followed up by colour studies, in whose complementary colour composition, avoiding local tone, the plastic body forms suddenly disappear. From Naturalism, the artist moves into a new dimension, researching into the artistic significance of coloured light. This virtually opened the way for Kupka's abstract painting, even though its detailed working out was to take a number of years yet. Nonetheless, Kupka never abandoned the path found at the beginning of the century. With increasingly firm conviction, and with more and more articulate means of expressing his meditative intuition, he raised rebellious individualism to the level of a demiurgic creator, 'allegorized' for him in the form of 'Prometheus'. Unlike most of his younger contemporaries, this intense creative approach never severed Kupka from the firm base of his experiences, which gave birth to 'Joys – A Ballad'. Through this continuity he showed his originality and his clairvoyance.

43.

František Kupka:
Corpse
1901, black chalk,
13.2 × 11.6 cm
K 40626 National
Gallery, Prague

44·

František Kupka:
Struggling
Anthropoids
Indian ink and white,
21.5 × 27.5 cm
G 2169 Regional
Gallery,
Hradec Králové

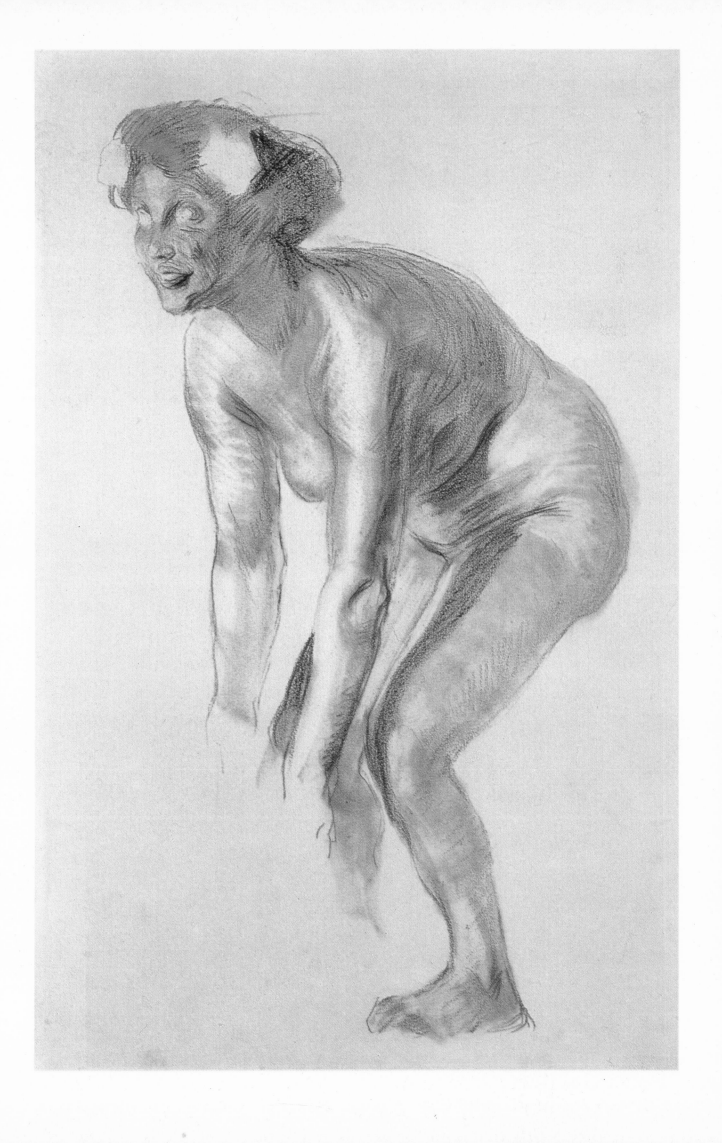

František Kupka:
Abstract
Composition
(Intensification)
*1920, Indian ink
and watercolour,
25.7 × 22.8 cm
K 35999 National
Gallery, Prague*

Auguste Rodin

The drawings of Auguste Rodin are inseparably linked with his work as a sculptor. This link, however, does not mean the drawing's direct dependence on his sculpture, because, on the whole, Rodin did not fashion his statues according to his drawings. The connection is more illuminating since it proves the exceptional inner maturity and creative sovereignty of Rodin's concept of art.

The master's drawings can roughly be divided into three large groups. The first comprises drawings from his youth, and from the period when he began to devote himself to the arts. The most interesting aspect of these drawings is their connection with Rodin's drawing teacher at the Petit Ecole, Horace Lecoq de Boisbaudran. His unorthodox and exceptionally inventive method, which, however, abided by the European tradition of draughtsmanship, particularly as it reached its most splendid chapter in the 18th century, has been held by the critic, A. Elsen, to have been a constant influence on Rodin's work.[25]

The second group of Rodin's drawings dates from the turn of the seventies and eighties and developed under the inspiration of Dante's 'Divine Comedy', from which Rodin derived his theme for his 'Gate of Hell', which, though never finished, forms the very backbone of his art. In these mixed, dramatic visions, freely selected from poetic themes of obscure encounters and mésalliances, with the repeated figure of the galloping rider, Ugolino, with man struggling with monsters, and with pictures of sinners suffering torment, all expressed in striking movement, Rodin's style of drawing crystallized. His drawing is 'sculptural' mainly in the sense that it concentrates on the main contours that define the bodies of the participants in movement, like sculptor's material in its basic volume, its components and its directions of movement, as in its 'profiles', which Rodin later frequently discussed with his literary friends and interpreters. His drawing is also 'sculptural' in the sense that it frees its maker from the duty of fulfilling the form-copying demands of academic drawing, for Rodin himself could treat his work as 'mere studies', as something very private, corresponding simply to the fantasy of their maker. The accepted territory of artistic sketches here served as a platform on which the artist penetrated to his own self, and from which he developed innovations inimical to the prevailing system of art.

The third and largest group of Rodin's drawings, which grew in scope from the nineties onwards, is entirely formed by female nudes, drawn in the most varied postures, particularly with dance movements and expressions. Rodin's style here became greatly simplified – he abandoned plastic shading and drew a single line with a pencil or a pen, over which he sometimes washed watercolour in flat patches covering the skin, hair or draperies, without paying scrupulous attention to the drawing below. These very simple drawings can be considered Rodin's greatest contribution to the art of drawing at the turn of the century, and even as an expression of one of the more substantial features of modern culture as it began to take shape.

The circumstances under which these drawings originated are well known. In his studio in the Hôtel Biron Rodin observed nude models moving freely about and studied dancers as they improvised, including such famous dancers as Isadora Duncan and Loie Fuller. Another time he studied a group of royal Cambodian dancing girls performing in complex, gesticulative ritual. He drew them as they moved without even as much as looking at the paper, letting one drawing after another drop onto the carpet, rather like a living movie camera. It certainly was no mere chance that the first, phased pictures of the movements of horses, and also of female nudes, originated in the same epoch (E. Muybridge) as the experiments that developed early cinematography and later excited the Italian Futurists. But the comparison ends there, for Rodin rejected photography, just as Gauguin had done. He was not at all concerned with 'scientific objectivity' in movement or even with the results of his work, that is, the individual drawings, although he did not like to part with these intimate souvenirs and exhibited them occasionally. The main thing for him was, apparently, the enjoyment derived from the source of the drawings themselves, the general psychic response of his personality reacting to the stimulus of natural reality: the moment in which he mobilized all his subjective faculties – the perceptive power of his eye, the nervous excitement, the skill of his hand to grasp and give expression to something that sprang from his emotions.

Rodin was often called an Impressionist, clearly because he stressed light in his sculpture, because of his frequent statements placing nature above tradition in the arts, and because of the late drawings of nudes. But not a single one of these aspects of Rodin's art is, properly speaking, Impressionist. Rodin felt light to be a significant contrast to shade, which he not only did not eliminate from his statues, but, indeed, elucidated as a symbolic theme in the well-known group in the 'Gate of Hell'. His gradual withdrawal from involvement with fantastic subjects, in fact, went far beyond Impressionism. The later Rodin did not really break continuity with the Symbolist ambitions of his Dantean visions, but on the contrary affirmed a certain polarity with his beginnings by giving it a new quality. It was characteristic of Rodin's first famous statue, his 'Bronze Age' (1876) that the sculptor could be accused of simply casting the living body of the Belgian soldier who stood model for him, so naturalistic was the effect of modelling the statue. On the other hand, there was a certain resonance from Michelangelo's 'Dying Slave' in the Louvre. Rodin's strong and constant interest in Michelangelo as the 'Last Gothic artist' made him appear as a renewer of the old gnostic-platonic tradition which gave symbolic treatment to the awakening from sleep as the return of the soul from the imprisonment of darkness and death to its original divine purpose.[26] He thus became the founder of a thematic order of 'somnambulant' motifs, later often to be used in Symbolism. His late works, particularly the drawings, integrated these two aspects into a closer correlation and interpenetration.

The motto of this development can be seen in 'Bronze Age' where dominant significance was attributed to anamnesis, or recollection, conceived as emotional participation. Recollection, of course, does not always have to refer to atavistic memories of the race, or to an individual's pre-natal memories, or to other fixations remote in time. It refers to the problem of memory generally, and comprises even the memory of things actually seen by the eye. After all, even Rodin's drawing teacher encouraged his pupils' personality by some kind of 'removal' of the model (Elsen), and its depiction with eyes closed. By this, and similar methods, he sought to stimulate the pupils' imagination in all respects and endow it with its own control.

In drawing, and in the free modelling of moving models, Rodin apparently found an ever more creative stimulus. His sculpture is generally characterized as a tragic depiction of the fate of man crushed by the magnitude of destiny. His 'Citizens of Calais', so imaginatively interpreted by Rilke, confirm this characteristic by pointing to the single psychological and moral value which is left to man in his encounter with death. But alongside this 'Christian' stoicism Rodin showed his other absorption – the sensuality reflected in Classical art. Rodin often 'embodied' these two elements by comparing his two ideals in art: Michelangelo and Pheidias. He aimed at achieving a new balance between these two contrasting qualities. Rodin was a supporter of the new synthesis, even though he clearly interpreted this in a slightly different way than, for example, his pupils.

The drawings of nudes are one of the clear legacies of this attempted synthesis by Rodin. Their 'instant' quality is far from being mere fragmentation. Rodin is, in reality, far closer to what was later called 'automatic drawing' than to Impressionism. The act of drawing, which is here practised on the intimately-known shape of the female body, involves the total concentration of all the abilities, knowledge and energy of its performer, who, in experiencing a sympathetic balancing between his personality and the female as representing 'human nature', moves from the dead calm of the academic pose to the inexhaustible wealth of living expression and movement, and reaches a degree of truthfulness in his representation that no Renaissance theoretician would have dared to dream of. At the same time, the artist goes beyond a traditional work of art with its limits of accepted meanings. Art thus becomes an aid to raising the intensity of a positive attitude to life in quite a new, modern, dynamic and practical sense.

47.

Auguste Rodin:
Mme Séverine
black chalk,
32.1 × 27 cm
1935-2767
Szépmüvészeti Museum
(Museum of Fine Arts),
Budapest

48.

Auguste Rodin:
Standing Nude
pencil, 23.8 × 16.8 cm
K 31655 National
Gallery, Prague

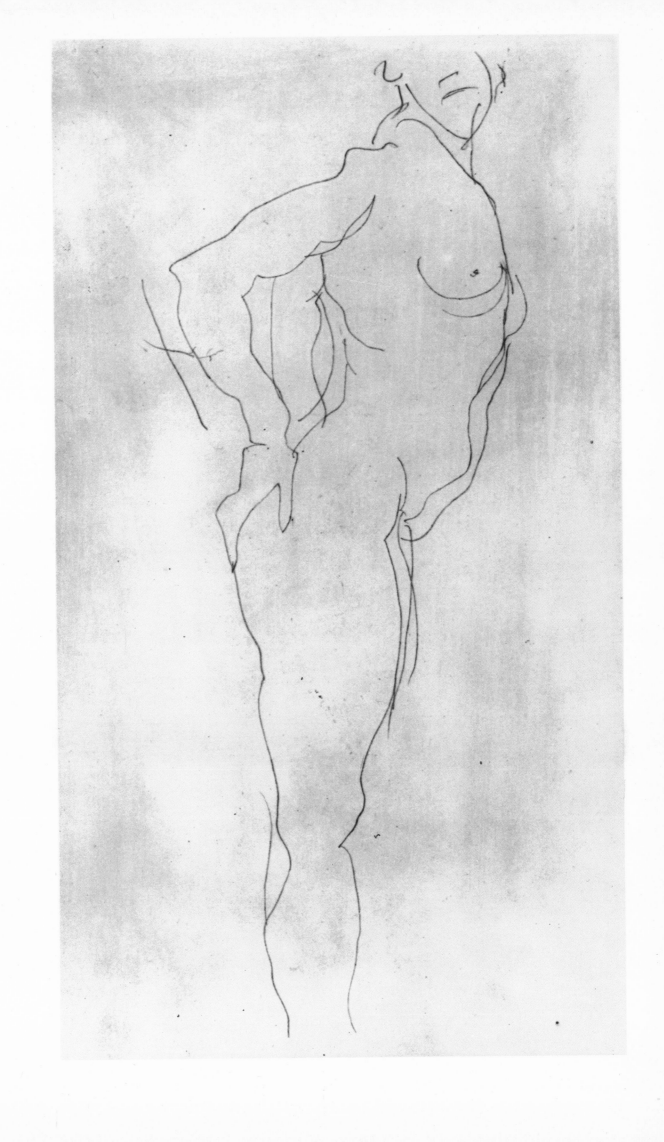

Gustav Klimt

Vienna was one of the most lively centres of European cultural life at the turn of the century. The *Wiener Sezession*, the association responsible for the ferment in the fine arts, had from 1897 fanned the flames of cultural activity, and, by holding exhibitions of its members and of leading representatives of the entire modern movement in Europe, had steadily prepared the ground for all the arts to flourish. The Vienna *Sezession* artists were influenced by developments in Belgium, England and Scotland, but their leading artists imbued their works with a specific, local charm, peculiar to the Viennese cultural milieu, where poetic levity and sentimentality, leavened with more abrasive admixtures, gave Viennese eroticism a markedly sophisticated character.

It was characteristic of the Vienna *Sezession* that it did not limit itself to art lovers, but sought to present its, at first sight, rather exclusive taste to a wider public. This public intention came about from the participation of a large number of architects in the development of the movement, but the basic tendency to consider all works of art, even the very intimate and exclusive kind, as public matter was fully held by the painters as well. The press in Vienna encouraged this enterprise, following cultural matters with great interest and adding strength to the existing traditions of public involvement in Viennese art.

If one studies the early work of the most important painter of the Vienna *Sezession*, Gustav Klimt, one is struck by the role the theatre played in it. Klimt's biggest commissions in the eighties were the paintings decorating the Karlovy Vary theatre, and the stairway of the Vienna Burgtheater. Here he was able fully to exhibit his exceptional skill and alertness as a painter; his masterly allegorical compositions and his portraits indicated that Klimt was to become a worthy successor to the highly popular Makart. Though Klimt deserted his popular brand of illusionism in the nineties, entered a period when he concentrated on light sfumato effects and came close to the new *Art Nouveau* stylization, his central attachment to the theatre did not at heart change. Later, Klimt's *Art Nouveau* work often roused furious opposition, but it seems that the 172,000 people who came to look at his pictures, 'Philosophy' and 'Medicine' (completed in 1900 and 1901 for the University of Vienna) appreciated the unusual Symbolist allegories and approved of the decorative and fictitious conception of a work of art.

In the nineties, Klimt first upset traditional, static allegorism by introducing into it everyday intimate scenes, e.g. 'Love' (1895), interpreting the emotional mood by means of form corroded by light. At the same time there was a call for 'painting ideas' which stressed the need for a style as a comprehensive expression of the artists' view of the world, and led the painters to the endeavour to share in creating a new total work of art (*Gesamtkunstwerk*). Klimt expressed this contradictory trend of the nineties in his allegory of the theatre as an actress in classical costume, holding a mask close to her face (*c.* 1895). He expressed this in even more precise style in the 'Allegory of Tragedy' (1897), which, interestingly, used a Japanese dragon motif. This dualism of the 'living' face and the mask seems to have attracted Klimt strongly, because he used a similar solution for the door lintel of the music room of 'Mr Dumb' (1898), depicting 'Music' as a compound of an ethereal but living woman, and of the non-living figure of a sphinx, set against a background of ingeniously primitive, already typically 'Klimtian' ornament. His big mural painting of 'Philosophy' was similarly conceived as a confrontation of the transitory nature of human life, developing from the innocence of childhood through love to the desperation of old age, with the contemplative, motionless face of the sphinx vanishing into the mists and cosmic distances of interstellar space.

The counterpart to this picture was 'Medicine'. In it, suffering mankind floated through the universe in somnambulant sleep. Here, however, in addition to the separate nude female figure, provocative and erotic in her vitality (known also from a drawing entitled 'Floating'), the figure of Hygeia appeared in the foreground, dressed as a priestess in richly-ornamented garments (in the drawing from the years 1897—98 she was depicted in a simple Greek robe), and with a spirally-twisted snake on her arm.

In these pictures, Klimt undoubtedly achieved Symbolist iconography with all its attributes and brought the Austrian movement to the same level as West European Symbolism. His specific contribution to the world of Symbolist pictorial images was a new version of the *femme fatale*. Klimt linked this type consistently with ornaments, even more than did Beardsley or Mucha. This image reached its zenith in the notorious 'Beethoven Frieze', a coloured drawing done on the occasion of an exhibition in honour of the composer, which the Vienna *Sezession* held in the year 1902 under the supervision of the architect Hoffmann. The centre-piece of this homage was a statue by Max Klinger, which mirrored the basic endeavour of the Vienna artists to disengage Man, through poetic and idealist gesture, from everyday reality, and raise him to pure being and beauty. It reflected this aim both in the ideal depiction of the musical genius sitting on a fantastic throne in a state of creative concentration, and in the actual composition of the statue itself, made of multi-coloured marble. The themes of Klimt's frieze were in full concord with this. For instance, under the title 'My Realm is not of this World' he depicted the mystical fusion of man and woman by the motif of a kiss of two nude figures encircled by ornamental compositions of stylized female figures. In another example, 'Longing for Happiness', he used the figure of a knight, an image popular among the Symbolists. Here, Klimt was truly not too far from that unity of figure and ornament that we know from the pictures of the Dutchmen, Johan Thorn Prikker and Jan Toorop, or that was practised by the members of the Glasgow School, and which appealed greatly to Viennese artists. But Klimt's own conception of this relationship developed differently, the result being the typical dualism of a naturalistic depiction of the bared parts of the body, with the rest of the picture covered with abstract ornament. Klimt's typical figural works from the first decade, which culminated in his famous 'Kiss' (1908–1911) – a mosaic in the Stoclet palace in Brussels built by Hoffmann – are all based on the provocative contradiction of emotional faces and sensitively expressive hands, filling large-size pictures, and the colourful and suggestive groupings of flat ornamental shapes enlivened with frequent spiral and eye motifs, recalling certain magnificent pagan mosaics of semi-precious stones and gold.

160

Klimt's blend of figure and ornament certainly tallied with the significance of ornament in *Art Nouveau* architecture of the time. Pictures and buildings formed an integral unit of style. Before long, however, this ornamentation was subjected to sharp comment in Vienna from Adolf Loos. His influential criticism led to the exclusion of all decorative elements from contemporary architecture and even brought about the fall of the artificial paradise that *Art Nouveau* artists had conjured up in their imaginary world. Naturally, Klimt came under pressure and, in 1909, he even stopped painting entirely for a whole year. Yet Klimt was a stubborn man and this pause could not have been caused only by external criticism. The truest explanation is that his art had reached the stage when every further step meant a major upheaval.

Klimt's use of decoration had deeper significance and meaning. Ornament in his work represented the cosmological element in the picture, expressed in illusive form in 'Philosophy'. The dualism of naturalistic, 'human' symbols and abstract ornament in Klimt's pictures formed a certain unity, which could be understood as an analogical response to those challenges that Nietzsche laid before the consciousness of the artistic world in his writings on the emergence of Greek tragedy from the spirit of music. Nietzsche saw the human artistic instinct as composed of two opposing elements: the Apollonian element, leading by way of dreams to the particularization of individual images in time and space, to figures, plastic works and the establishment of the entire world of semblance; and the mystical, Dionysian element, which renders proof of the mystery of the world, as seen in non-objective music. Similarly, Klimt's pictures, which were conceived in the Nietzschean spirit as symbols of a valid and unified vision of the world, evoked through the duality of individual plastic detail and abstract, flat ornament the basic philosophical idea of the necessary correlation of the original substance of the world and individual human destiny. In this manner, Klimt painted Salome and Judith with the severed head of Holophernes as typical themes of such tragic notions. The provocative attraction of these pictures arose not only from the immediate contrast of concrete and abstract shapes, but also from the fact that these values were, to a large extent, reversible. The eroticism and extreme emotionality of the human forms spoke out in favour of Dionysus, as much as the Symbolist features of the ornament echoed Apollo's ability to give shape – but the charm of the shining colours and gold reigned supreme.

This type of composition, perfect in its way, was, in reality, very artificial and, as became apparent in Klimt's portraits of ladies commissioned by rich Viennese sitters, was becoming a fashionable theme. What was meant as unity disintegrated again. But it was the core of Nietzsche's teaching that the two basic forces of the creative instinct could not be separated, in spite of all their differences.[27] Klimt must have felt the same, if we consider the continuity of the theme of 'The Kiss' throughout his work. Klimt's crisis was, undoubtedly, caused by the urgently-felt need for the greater integration of the two basic elements in his pictorial composition, a longing for a greater fusion in their totality.

This new trend in Klimt's work resulted in many drawings. The vast quantity of Klimt's pencil sketches shows that he abandoned ornament, and concentrated on the immediate experience of vital perception, exemplified by his studies of the bodies of beautiful women. The new corporeality of Klimt's vision, which, in its sensuality, ignored all the moral structures of the old, didactic art, was not simply a question of getting closer to painting, as a belated reaction to French post-Impressionist painting, nor was it evidence that the artist's personality was disintegrating. The two striking structural aspects of this large set of drawings – on the one hand, their pan-eroticism and, on the other, the fact that their style became increasingly authentically 'Klimtian' – prove that, in them, Klimt found a new unity, born, nevertheless, in a spirit close to Nietzsche. In these drawings, Klimt reached that 'immediate certainty of viewpoint' which, according to Nietzsche, made art a specific key to a new understanding of the world.

50.

Gustav Klimt:
Standing Nude
c. 1900, black chalk,
44 × 32.7 cm
K 8702 National
Gallery, Prague

Nachlaß meines Bruders Gustav
Hermine Klimt

51.

Gustav Klimt:
Design drawing
for 'Philosophy'
1898/99,
black chalk and pencil,
89.6 × 63.2 cm
71506 Historisches
Museum der Stadt
Wien, Vienna

Gustav Klimt:
Reclining Nude
Girls with Stockings
c. 1900, pencil,
35.1 × 55.1 cm
K 7463 National
Gallery, Prague

53·

Gustav Klimt:
Lady with Bared
Breasts
1907/08, pencil,
blue and red crayon,
54.7 × 36 cm
Graphische Sammlung
Albertina, Vienna

54·

Gustav Klimt:
Seated Girl
Wearing a Hat
pencil and red crayon,
56 × 37 cm
K 17444 National
Gallery, Prague

55.

Gustav Klimt:
Reclining Woman
pencil, 37.4 × 57 cm
private collection,
Prague

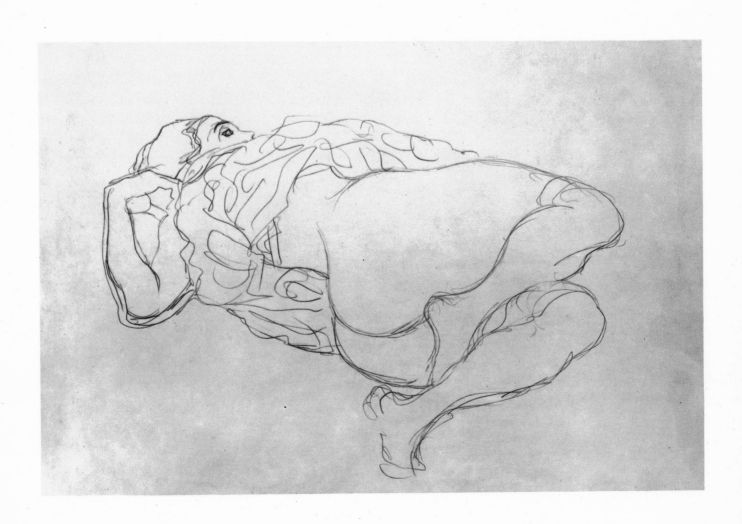

56.

Gustav Klimt:
Three Sitting
Female Nudes
c. 1907, pencil,
56.5 × 37 cm
K 17442 National
Gallery, Prague

GVSTAV
KLIMT
NACHLASS

57.

Gustav Klimt:
Female Portrait
c. 1917, pencil,
57 × 37.5 cm
K 17445 National
Gallery, Prague

Egon Schiele

Egon Schiele's work, properly speaking, stands outside art at the turn of the century, for he studied at the Vienna Academy as late as 1906—1909. And yet the general character of his work, as well perhaps as the date of his premature death in 1918, seems to bring to a close the epoch of fundamental change which we have been tracing in the art of several of its outstanding figures.

Schiele's work, culminating in his watercolours and gouache drawings, can, to a considerable extent, be considered the final chapter of art at the turn of the century, particularly as exemplifying the psychological profile of the artist in this profoundly individualistic period. Schiele's work, concentrated and simplified down to its bare essence, reveals the attitude which art around 1900 bequeathed to later artists. This standpoint was for a time masked, for example by the utopian optimism and ardour for reform of the inter-war avant-gardes, but its roots continued to grow and came to the surface in the assessment of the state of profound crisis, in which contemporary society found itself.

Klimt's influence on Schiele was considerable. Indeed, even though Schiele had abandoned the use of ornamental elements in his pictures, his manner of siting the figure in the format of the canvas, or paper, was still 'decorative' in a Klimtian way. Schiele, similarly, employed the contradiction of expressively stressed faces and hands, with bodies spread over the entire surface. This can best be seen where they were covered by draperies given in deeper colour tones, their areas contrasting with the more plastically conceived skin parts, which are given in a bluish shade. Schiele's figures fill the surface, as did Klimt's, but, instead of a richly ornamented setting, they are surrounded only by empty white paper, and so appear smaller and more fragile.

This can be seen as early as in the 'Portrait of E. Kosmack', dating from 1910 (today in the Österreichische Galerie in Vienna), which has a square format in the style of Klimt. But this equal-sided shape is not employed harmoniously, for the large area of the background stands out against the dark contour of the small frontal figure with a large head, and this lack of proportion gives the picture a quite novel, dramatic effect. These changes are meant expressly to add significance. In the work of Klimt, the female figure, in emotional tension shown in the blissfully half-closed eyes and fusion with the ornament, deliberately merged with the assumed 'original base' of the world. Schiele's sharply-outlined little figures, which increasingly became more and more inturned and which, for the greater part, are self-portraits and figures of men, do not entirely extricate themselves from this basic ontological correlation, which, here and there, upholds the entire artistic view, although their emotional fusion is entirely painful. There is an awareness of an imaginary barrier between the individual and the unit of the world, which is very difficult to overcome. In another drawing, from 1912, which represents the artist sitting in prison wearing a red coat, Schiele added: 'I love contradictions'.

Schiele was strongly affected by the prevailing neuroses which underlay art at the turn of the century. The representatives of modern art in the nineties had responded to this pressure by objectivization, which formed a new, artistic *univers discours*. We indicated this in the introduction by our example of a triangle of mutually complementary, naturalistic, decorative-ornamental and fantastic-symbolical trends. This configuration, though rather arbitrary at first sight, covered fairly exhaustively the basic symbolic functions that art had to perform, if it wished to find its place as a historically valid cultural phenomenon. The new art, though, was still too disparate; and, as the 20th century advanced, the need for considerable concentration of art form and for an internal integration of individual trends increased. Great belief in the fundamental capacity of artistic intuition, and the various trends towards mysticism arising from this, led the artists working around 1900 to stress emotionality as decisive, even in the arts. The sudden collapse of *Art Nouveau* ornamentalism can hardly be explained otherwise than by the fact that this antimorphological viewpoint assumed a leading role in the evaluation of artistic values. Ornament, of course, meant more than decorativeness and decoration – it was a symbol comprising the whole of culture in its Apollonian element. It demanded a homogeneity of style in the living, as in the spiritual, environment. When, however, the younger generation of Viennese artists, for example, abandoned it in favour of the more basic structural contradictions, the heterogeneity that creates life and art, they probably did not realize that, instead of a basic change, a mere shift had occurred, or else simply a greater concentration of the original alignments. Masks were removed and, for example, in Schiele's sensitive drawings, the torment of existence was laid bare, sparking off in the contradictions of inward-turned eroticism and secularized religiosity a flame of sacred fear and modern 'cramped beauty'. This new authenticity, however, at once became conscious of the void around it, and was, thus, faced with the demand that some new 'ornament' should be created which would gain a general hearing for the loneliness of its truthful experience.

58.

Egon Schiele:
Design drawing
for the Portrait
of E. Kosmack
1911, pencil,
41.6 × 33.5 cm
private collection,
Prague

S 1911.

Egon Schiele:
Sitting Female Nude
*1912, pencil and red
crayon, 48 × 32 cm
private collection,
Prague*

Egon Schiele:
Reclining Woman
with Auburn Hair
1917,
pencil and gouache,
46 × 29.5 cm
K 17863 National
Gallery, Prague

Egon Schiele:
Seated Nude Woman
1917, black chalk,
46 × 29.5 cm
K 17862 National
Gallery, Prague

62.

Egon Schiele:
The Artist's Wife
1917,
pencil and gouache,
46 × 30.5 cm
K 17864 National
Gallery, Prague

Egon Schiele:
Self-Portrait
c. 1917,
pencil and gouache,
46 × 30.5 cm
K 17865 National
Gallery, Prague

1. W. Hofmann: *Von der Nachahmung zur Erfindung der Wirklichkeit – Die schöpferische Befreiung der Kunst 1890—1917.* Cologne 1970.

2. R. Schmutzler: *Nouveau Art – Jugendstil.* Stuttgart 1962, p. 35 and 109 ff.

3. A. Hauser: *Mannerism I—II The Crisis of the Renaissance and the Origin of Modern Art.* London 1965, p. 358 ff.

4. S. Mallarmé: *Réponse à une enquête.* In: J. Huret: *Sur l'évolution littéraire,* Paris 1891.

5. B. Reade: *Art Nouveau and Alphonse Mucha.* London 1963, p. 18.

6. J. Mucha: *Can-can with a Halo.* Prague 1969, p. 158.

7. Ibid., p. 171 ff.

8. Mario Praz: *Liebe, Tod und Teufel – Die schwarze Romantik.* Munich 1970.

9. B. Reade: *Aubrey Beardsley.* New York 1967.

10. A. Koestler: *The Act of Creation.* New York 1967, p. 27 ff.

11. S. Sandström: *Le monde imaginaire d'Odilon Redon.* Lund 1955.

12. K. Berger: *Odilon Redon.* Cologne 1964.

13. Ibid.

14. R. A. Heller: *The Riddle of Edvard Munch's Sphinx.* In: Paper from the Xth AICA Congress at the Munch-museet, Oslo, August 29, 1969.

15. Note on the picture 'Despair' in the property of the Munch-Museet, Oslo.

16. O. Benesch: *Edvard Munch's Glaube* – Edvard Munch 100 är. In: Kommunes Kunstsamlinger – Arbok 1963, Oslo 1963, p. 102 ff.

17. Oscar Wilde: *De Profundis.* London 1909, pp. 85 and 75.

18. *Poet and Sculptor* – The Letters of J. Zeyer and F. Bílek. Published by J. R. Marek, Prague 1948. (In Czech.)

19. Ibid, p. 208.

20. O. Březina: *The Only Work.* In: Volné směry 9, 1909, p. 69. (In Czech.)

21. W. Winkler: *Das Oneroid* – Zur Psychose Alfred Kubins. In: Archiv für Psychiatrie, 1948, p. 136 ff.

22. E. W. Bredt: *Alfred Kubin,* Munich 1922, p. 102-108.

23. L. Vachtová: *František Kupka,* Prague 1968, p. 66 and 67. (In Czech.)

24. Ibid, p. 38.

25. A. Elsen: *Rodin.* New York 1963, p. 160 ff.

26. M. Eliade: *Aspects du mythe.* Paris 1963, p. 156.

27. E. Fink: *Nietzsches Philosophie.* Stuttgart 1960, p. 20 ff.

ALFONS MUCHA, b. 1860 at Ivančice in Moravia; 1879—81 painted stage decorations in Vienna: 1883—87 studied at the Munich Academy, 1887 attended the Julian Academy in Paris; from 1889 resident in Paris, 1894 first poster for Sarah Bernhardt; 1903 and 1909 in the U.S.A., 1910 returned to his native country; died in Prague in 1939.
Literature: B. Reade: *Art Nouveau and Alphonse Mucha*, London 1963
J. Mucha: *Can-can with a Halo*, Prague 1969

AUBREY VINCENT BEARDSLEY, b. 1872 in Brighton, England; 1892 left an insurance office and devoted himself to the arts; 1894 illustrated O. Wilde's *Salome* and became the artistic director of the journal *The Yellow Book;* died at Menton in 1898.
Literature: B. Reade: *Aubrey Beardsley*, New York 1967

ODILON REDON, b. 1840 at Bordeaux, France; 1855 studied at St. Gorin; 1870 moved to Paris; 1879 published his first album, 'In a Dream'; 1886 met Gauguin and exhibited at the Salon of the Twenty in Brussels; 1897 sold the farm at Peyrelebade; 1904 entire hall at the Autumn Salon given over to his work; died in Paris in 1916.
Literature: A. Mellerio: *Odilon Redon: Peintre, Dessinateur et Graveur*, Paris 1923
Sandström: *Le Monde imaginaire d'Odilon Redon*, Lund 1955
K. Berger: *Odilon Redon*, Cologne 1964

EDVARD MUNCH, b. 1863 at Løten, Norway; 1881—84 studied at the Academy in Oslo; 1885, 1889, 1891 visits to Paris; 1898—1908 visits to Germany; 1908 nervous breakdown; 1909—15 mural paintings for the University of Oslo; died at Ekely in 1944.
Literature: J. H. Langaard and R. Revold: *The Drawings of Edvard Munch*, Oslo 1958
G. Svenaeus: *Edvard Munch, Das Universum der Melancholie*, Lund 1968

JAN PREISLER: b. 1872 at Popovice, Bohemia; 1887—95 studied at the School of Applied Arts in Prague; member of the Mánes Association in Prague; from 1913 on Professor at the Prague Academy; died in Prague in 1918.
Literature: A. Matějček: *Jan Preisler*, Prague 1960
J. Kotalík: *Jan Preisler*, Prague 1968

FRANTIŠEK BÍLEK, b. 1872 at Chýnov, Bohemia; 1887 and 1890 studied at the Prague Academy; 1891 at the Académie Collarosi in Paris; 1909 publication of his book, *The Way;* died at Chýnov in 1941.
Literature: Fr. Kovárna: *František Bílek*, Prague 1941

ALFRED KUBIN, b. 1877 at Litoměřice, Bohemia; 1891—92 attended the School of Arts-and-Crafts at Salzburg; 1892—96 apprentice to a photographer at Klagenfurth; 1898—1901 studied at the Academy in Munich; 1906 moved to Zwickledt; 1908 wrote the novel, *Die andere Seite;* 1912 member of the group Der Blaue Reiter; 1937 Professor at the Viennese Academy; died at Zwickledt in 1959.
Literature: P. F. Schmidt: *Alfred Kubin*, Leipzig 1924
W. Schmied: *Alfred Kubin*, Salzburg 1967

FRANTIŠEK KUPKA, b. 1871 at Opočno, Bohemia; 1888 studied at the Prague Academy; 1892 moved to the Viennese Academy; 1895 moved to Paris and became a well-known illustrator; 1912 exhibited his abstract Two-Coloured Fugue at the Autumn Salon; 1931 elected to the presidium of the association Abstraction-Création; died at Puteaux in 1957.
Literature: L. Vachtová: *František Kupka*, Prague 1968

AUGUSTE RODIN, b. 1840 in Paris; 1854 entered the Ecole imperiale de Dessin et de Mathématique in Paris; 1857 failed to pass the entrance examination to the Ecole des Beaux Arts; 1871 left for Belgium; 1880 commission for the entrance gate to the projected Museum of Decorative Arts; 1898 scandal around the Balzac Monument; 1900 special pavilion at the World Exhibition; died at Meudon in 1917.
Literature: A. Elsen: *Rodin*, New York 1963

GUSTAV KLIMT, b. 1862 at Baumgarten, Austria; 1876—83 studied at the
School of Arts-and-Crafts in Vienna; 1897 first president of the association Wiener
Sezession; 1905 left the association; died in Vienna in 1918.
Literature: E. Pirchan: *Gustav Klimt*, Vienna 1956
         J. Dobai – F. Novotny: *Gustav Klimt*, Salzburg 1967

EGON SCHIELE, b. 1890 at Tulln on the Danube; 1906—09 studied at the
Vienna Academy; 1914 enlisted in the army; died in Vienna in 1918.
Literature: E. Mitsch: *Egon Schiele*, Salzburg 1961

TABLE OF ILLUSTRATIONS